Healthcare Spaces

Roger Yee

No.5

Healthcare Spaces

Roger Yee

No.5

Visual Profile Books Inc., New York

Opposite: University of Arkansas for Medical Sciences, Bed Tower and Parking Garage Design firm: HKS, Inc. Photography: Ed LaCasse

Healthcare Spaces No. 5

302 Fifth Avenue • New York, NY 10001
Tel: 212.279.7000 • Fax: 212.279.7014

www.visualreference.com

PUBLISHER	Larry Fuersich larry@visualreference.com
EDITORIAL DIRECTOR	Roger Yee rhtyee@gmail.com
CREATIVE ART DIRECTOR	Martina Parisi martina@visualreference.com
PRODUCTION MANAGER	John Hogan johnhvrp@yahoo.com
CONTROLLER	Angie Goulimis angie@visualreference.com

ISBN 13: 978-0-9825989-6-2
ISBN 10: 0-9825989-6-3

Distributors to the trade in the United States and Canada
Innovative Logistics
575 Prospect Street
Lakewood, NJ 08701
732.363.5679

Distributors outside the United States and Canada
HarperCollins International
10 East 53rd Street
New York, NY 10022-5299

Exclusive distributor in China
Beijing Designerbooks Co., Ltd.
B-0619, No.2 Building, Dacheng International Center
78 East 4th Ring Middle Road
Chaoyang District, Beijing 100022, P.R. China
Tel: 0086(010)5962-6195 Fax: 0086(010)5962-6193
E-mail: info@designerbooks.net www.designerbooks.net

Printed and bound in China

Book Design: Martina Parisi

The paper on which this book is printed contains recycled content to support a sustainable world.

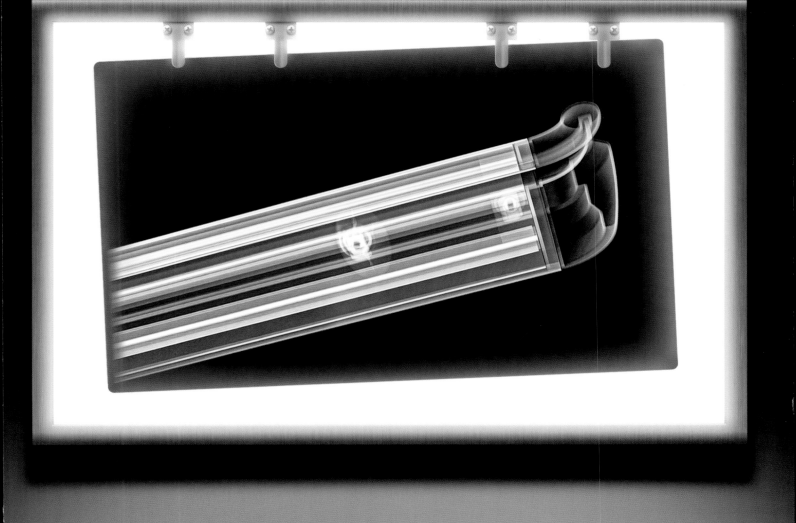

Test Results: Totally free from PVC and PBTs

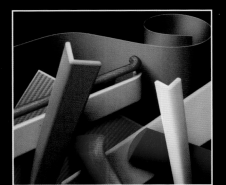

Introducing New Acrovyn® 4000. Who says you can't protect your walls and the building's occupants at the same time? After years of research and testing, we've totally reengineered the world's best wall protection. You get Acrovyn's legendary durability and good looks free from PVC and persistent bioaccumulative toxins—*all for no extra cost!* To learn more about New Acrovyn 4000, visit www.c-sgroup.com, call 888-621-3344 or find Construction Specialties on ![f], ![in] or ![t] twitter.com/acrovyn.

 Acrovyn® *Protection for tomorrow's environment*

HEALTHCARE FURNITURE SOLUTIONS

FOR PATIENTS, FAMILY AND STAFF

PATIENT ROOM • BARIATRIC • PEDIATRIC • SLEEPOVER

WAITING & LOUNGE • TRAINING & CONFERENCE • DINING

SYSTEMS & DESKING • ADMINISTRATION • FILING & STORAGE

To learn more about
our healthcare
furniture solutions, visit
www.kihealthcare.com
or call 1-800-424-2432.

Furnishing Knowledge

arcadia

Designed by David Dahl

Rest at ease in a sanctuary of understated elegance with Haven, a comprehensive offering of seating and table products designed specifically with healthcare in mind. Guest and lounge models feature a passive flex back, clean-out portals as well as a range of replaceable components—from arm caps and complete arm frames to seat and back upholstery covers— to ensure lasting beauty and timeless satisfaction. Combine that with an assortment of aesthetic and multifunctional options and Haven becomes an infinitely purposeful, exceptionally durable collection that provides a lifetime of solace.

Contents

Introduction by Roger Yee   10

Architects & Interior Designers

Anderson Mikos Architects Ltd.   17
Array Healthcare Facilities Solutions   25
Ascension Group Architects   33
Cannon Design   41
Christner, Inc.   49
Earl Swensson Associates, Inc.   57
Ellerbe Becket, an AECOM Company   65
Ewingcole   73
FORMA Design   81
Francis Cauffman   89
HDR Architecture, Inc   97
Health Facilities Group   105
HGA Architects and Engineers   113
HKS   121
HMC Architects   129
HOK   137
Horty Elving   145
Jain Malkin, Inc.   153
Mitchell Associates   161
NBBJ   169
PageSoutherlandPage   177
Perkins Eastman   185
Perkins+Will   193
RTKL   201
Sparling   209
TAYLOR   217
WHR Architects   225
Wilmot Sanz, Inc.   233

Landscape Architects   241
Dirtworks Landscape Architecture, PC   243
Mahan Rykiel Associates   251

Wayfinding Designers   259
FMG Design, Inc.   261
Mitchell Associates   269

Index by Project   278

Introduction

Are You Feeling Better?

How design is improving the healthcare experience—in measurable ways—for patients, families and caregivers alike

By Roger Yee

A busy mother checks her to-do list before leaving Walmart and realizes there's enough time to take little Suzy to have her sore throat examined at the store's health clinic. That's right: Walmart. Big box retail stores, pharmacies and supermarkets are making room for clinics where nurse practitioners or physicians' assistants will see you without an appointment for about $60 (excluding tests) payable in cash or health insurance. Hundreds of thousands of Americans are visiting some 1,200 such facilities across the country annually, with some 61.3 percent having no family doctor to turn to, according to a 2008 Rand Corp. study. Useful as these clinics clearly are, they typically occupy no-frills spaces. Like the retail environments that surround them, they are clean, bright and orderly, probably all that patients expect for 15-minute consultations.

Welcome to 21st-century healthcare in the United States. With federal reform of healthcare having made a formal start with the passage of an historic bill in March 2010, the nation can look forward to a time when 95 percent of Americans will have health insurance coverage, many of the most egregious practices of the insurance industry will be curtailed, and cost control measures will help contain an annual healthcare bill that now exceeds $2.4 trillion—over 16 percent of gross domestic product—while leaving some 50 million people without coverage. As the retail health clinics demonstrate, the delivery of services will be distributed through new as well as established channels besides hospitals and doctors' offices, as the nation strives to match

supply to demand. Meanwhile, the design of healthcare facilities is making great strides in providing a better experience of health care for patients, their families and caregivers alike, wherever they are.

Why does it matter that more effective healing environments are being designed to enhance the healthcare experience? Accumulating documentation and growing acceptance of the theory of psychoneuro-immunology, which assigns a role to the emotions in the pathogenesis of physical diseases associated with immunological

Good wayfinding helps hospitals welcome families as partners in caregiving. This pedestrian bridge provides a distinctive link to the Quentin & Elisabeth Alexander NICU at Rainbow Babies & Children's Hospital, a unit of Cleveland's University Hospitals, designed by Array Healthcare Facilities Solutions.

dysfunctions, has enabled healthcare decisionmakers to appreciate and promote the connection between physical spaces designed to reduce stress and improved medical outcomes. In turn, our understanding of psychoneuroimmunology's implications have paved the way for over 1,500 evidence-based studies of the ways design can lower medical errors, infections and falls as well as relieve fear, discomfort and stress, giving architects and interior designers a baseline of measurable results for applying the lessons of good healthcare design.

Better yet, each new design innovation, once proven to be effective, empowers successive evidence-based design teams to make further advances, often through Pebble Projects promoted by the Center for Health Design, a respected, non-profit research and advocacy organization that has long championed design as a means to improve health care. (Institutions that participate in Pebble Projects collect data to measure the benefits of design interventions.) Though healthcare professionals and their design teams rightly state much remains to be done— the vital connections between LEED (Leadership in Energy and Environmental Design) and evidence-based design, for example, are largely unrealized at this point—progress can already be seen in the new generation of healthcare facilities.

For a look at the current healthcare experience of patients, patients' families and caregivers, *HEALTHCARE SPACES* has been fortunate to share the observations of Sherri R. Bowman, vice president and principal of Array Healthcare Facilities Solutions, in King of Prussia, Pennsylvania,

Design with light.

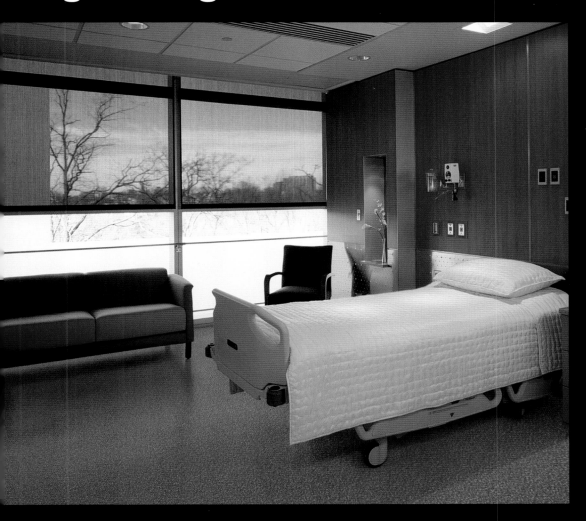

and her colleague, Patricia Malick, AAHID, EDAC, practice area leader/interior design, Cyndi McCullough, RN, vice president and senior healthcare consultant at HDR Architecture, in Omaha, and Jain Malkin, president of Jain Malkin Inc., in San Diego. What they report is truly encouraging. Design is making a significant contribution to health care, and the results can be measured and replicated everywhere.

The patient experience: Look who's got the remote!

Because major strides in healthcare design began with recognition of the validity of patient-centered care, it is reassuring to know that today's patient experience reflects design innovations found to help patients recover faster and more effectively. Facilities designed to support patient-centered care are letting patients exercise greater control over the healthcare environment while remaining more in touch with the outside world. As a result, they enable patients to overcome feelings of fear, disorientation, helplessness and isolation to significantly reduce stress levels.

Cyndi McCullough of HDR remembers the research she conducted as a nurse working with transplants at Omaha's Clarkson Hospital that helped establish the validity of patient-centered care by linking it to improved outcomes. "Although the research took a long time, it let us create a continuum within the healing environment, from the choice of paint colors to the delivery of care," she observes. "We found that doing good things for patients in terms of safety, privacy and comfort not only involved costs, they produced measurable benefits."

The impact of design on today's patient experience is readily apparent in the best examples of today's patient room. Having a private room, as Jain Malkin points out, removes a major psychological stressor— the intrusive presence of another patient— even as it reduces infection rates. In addition, remote controls for lighting, TV and room service, storage and display space for personal belongings, comfortable, residential-style furnishings, direct exposure to natural light and views, and proximity to bathroom over non-skid flooring all enhance the patient's sense of wellbeing through control of the environment, opportunities for customization, and

contact with nature and the surrounding neighborhood. Malkin notes that today's patient room owes much to the Planetree Model Hospital Project, which dates back to the 1970s and lets the patient exercise choice in nurturing care, active involvement, family participation and privacy, and the labor/delivery/recovery/postpartum (LDRP) room, which became popular in the 1990s and permits the mother to remain in one place when giving birth as people and services are brought to her.

Less obvious yet welcome are changes in the design of examination and treatment rooms that introduce patient-centered features. The newest examination rooms are not so strict about minimizing floor area, according to Array's Patricia Malick. "A bigger examination room brings many caregivers into the space, along with a family member, to deal with the patient in a more holistic way and not require the patient to move among different treatment modalities," she says. "There's also seating for a face-to-face discussion, which is more dignified and focused for the patient than being addressed on an examination table." Treatment rooms such as those for oncologic therapies often address the patient's anxiety with nature and artwork that provide distraction and relaxation.

The patient's family experience: No longer in the way?

Older visitors entering the current generation of hospitals notice the change in mood long before they enter a patient's room. "Being encouraged to partner with the hospital staff as caregivers is a major development for families," Malkin observes. "This is most noticeable in the patient room,

The stressful nature of healthcare occupations is inspiring healthcare institutions to provide more dedicated areas for staff. Shown here is a tranquil staff dining room at University of South Florida's Johnnie B. Byrd Sr. Alzheimer's Center & Research Institute, in Tampa, designed by HDR Inc.

which is now zoned so family members can be present without compromising care or staff." Staffing shortages are not the only motivation for recognizing the vital role families can play. "Since Medicare will not pay if a patient returns in less than 30 days with complications associated with the hospital stay or poor discharge planning," Malkin explains, "hospitals want to be sure someone besides the patient knows what's ahead in terms of medication and other important issues, especially when the patient is being discharged."

Given what can happen to a patient during a stay and after being discharged, frequently before being completely healed, hospitals are understandably happy to recruit family members as patient advocates. "There is much more emphasis lately on discharge planning," she states. "Follow-up calls to patients may reveal that prescriptions for important medications may not have been filled because the patient couldn't afford it or perhaps the patient did not understand the proper sequencing of several medications. All of this can lead to re-hospitalization or an expensive trip to the emergency room."

Welcoming family members as partners in caregiving and patients' advocates, healthcare institutions are making a sincere effort to support their expanded presence with better wayfinding, improved food services, attractive gift shops and other

retail stores, family-oriented private spaces and semi-private areas in public spaces, medical resource centers, chapels and even residential-style overnight accommodations. Families are thus discovering that many of their everyday needs have been anticipated to help them focus on patient care, as Array's Sherri Bowman can attest. "The most forward-thinking institutions are mapping the sequence of events from the moment patients and their families arrive to check in," she says. "By becoming more hospitable, they let you know you belong here."

The medical staff's experience: When caregivers need care

Generations before patient-centered care was even a topic of discussion, hospitals and other healthcare institutions traditionally designed their facilities based on what doctors, nurses and other medical personnel requested to do their jobs. Yet today's healthcare design is actually more effective in serving the staff, because it pays attention to the health, safety, efficiency and effectiveness of the overall healing environment and the physical and emotional toll it exacts, as well as the staff's specific shopping lists for space and equipment. The changes in corridors, nurses' stations, doctor's offices and other staff areas may not be as visually striking as those in the patient room, but they can profoundly affect job performance. "When you have what you need to do your job, when you can walk shorter distances, or when you find supplies right where they should be," McCullough suggests, "you feel you could easily work another shift."

Technology and design are combining in countless ways to produce important innovations that raise staff productivity and lower stress. For example, ceiling lifts not only help safely move patients to and from their beds, they reduce injury and lower insurance rates, while sinks located in the doorways to patient rooms make hand washing convenient and routine, linen carts with weight sensors can signal

Evidence-based design cites the private patient room for improving medical outcomes. This patient room in the Greg and Stacey Renker Pavilion at Eisenhower Medical Center, in Rancho Mirage, California, was designed by Jain Malkin Inc. to provide the best possible experience for inpatients and their families.

when it's time to restock, and patient-tracking systems let staff members know exactly where their patients are. Healthcare designers have learned that even minor adjustments in design can have major consequences for operations. Just placing a caregiver station equipped with keyboard and monitor outside a patient room lets a nurse quickly make direct observations, take notes and call up data without disturbing the patient.

Of course, much of the drive to improve staff accommodations comes from the realization among medical institutions and the public alike that healthcare is a highly stressful occupation. "How does our society expect nurses to work 12-hour shifts with half-hour lunch breaks?" asks Malkin. "Nursing could be the most stressful job on earth." While healthcare institutions may not be prepared to remedy such situations through extensive reforms, providing offstage lounges, dining rooms, meditation areas and fitness rooms can help—backed by the understanding that long-term solutions remain ahead.

Charting tomorrow's healthcare experience

Much remains to be done, nonetheless, to improve the healthcare experience. "We pick our targets whenever we're doing a project," McCullough reports. "There are always opportunities to make a difference. Everyone is looking for better performance, lower costs, fewer injuries and improved outcomes." But she cautions that design innovations must be firmly linked to daily

operations to succeed. "Putting a sink in the right place won't help," she maintains, "if the staff doesn't use it properly."

Our experts are unanimous on this point. In effect, the healthcare environment must be a physical extension of healthcare practice. "If you try to implement change with an outmoded healthcare facility," Malick insists, "the environment becomes one more burden to overcome." At the same time, she concedes, "A progressive environment only sets the stage. It can't work if the staff is not trained or motivated to change the culture."

In addition, designers cannot design forward-thinking healthcare environments without sympathetic healthcare administrators and practitioners to support them. Malkin cites architect Derek Parker, FAIA, RIBA, FACHA, a director of Anshen + Allen, who maintains that good design needs good clients. "What we seek are hospitals with great leadership teams, ready to reorganize themselves to create great healthcare experiences," she concludes. "That's how we'll ensure there's no sharp fall off as soon as we go past all those nice new lobbies."

Integra®

COASTAL

COLLECTION

HEALTHCARE ENVIRONMENTS
RECEPTION • WAITING • LOUNGE

800.235.0234   INTEGRASEATING.COM

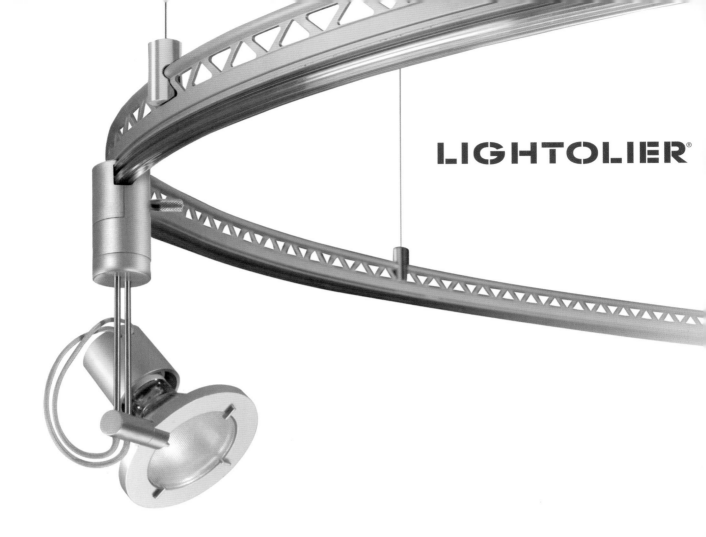

Anderson Mikos Architects, ltd.

Anderson Mikos Architects, ltd.

Rush-Copley Healthcare Center
Yorkville, Illinois

Great medical campuses, like mighty oaks, often begin as modestly as the recently completed first phase of Rush Copley Healthcare Center, in Yorkville, Illinois, designed by Anderson Mikos Architects. This award-winning, three-story, 58,200-square-foot ambulatory care facility simultaneously functions as a complete building and future hospital core on its 40-acre greenfield site. To handle non-life threatening injuries and ailments, it provides a 5,000-square-foot ambulatory care suite, 6,000-square-foot diagnostic and treatment center and 1,000-square-foot laboratory, along with a 28,200-square-foot medical office space. Key public and support facilities such as the main lobby, conference center and curving, single-loaded corridor represent tomorrow's main visitor and outpatient corridor. (Rush-Copley is now authorized to add an emergency department.) The horizontal masonry structure, inspired by the Prairie-style architecture of Frank Lloyd Wright, fits graciously into the community, anchored by an iconic tower that commands attention on a busy thoroughfare. Inside, the Prairie theme continues with warm earthtones, patterned terrazzo floors, and furnishings characterized by cherry wood, patterned upholstery, etched glass, solid-core countertops and richly detailed wallcoverings. Noting public acclaim for the Center, Lynn Dubajic, executive director of Yorkville Economic Development Corp., observes, "This new Rush-Copley complex will have a great positive impact here."

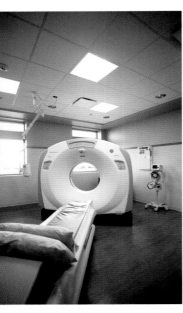

Far left, left: CT scan, urgent care treatment

Below left, below: Public corridor, exterior

Opposite: Main lobby

Photography: Courtesy of Leopardo Construction Company

Anderson Mikos Architects, ltd.

Advocate Condell Medical Center
Emergency Department Expansion and Renovation
Libertyville, Illinois

Aware of the typical patient's unsettling visit to an ER, Advocate Condell Medical Center, a 257-bed short-term hospital in Libertyville, Illinois, has expanded and renovated its emergency department to redefine the relationship of patients and their families with Condell's staff. The newly reopened facility, designed by Anderson Mikos Architects, reshapes the patient experience from the patient's perspective. As a result, the two-level, 43,000-square-foot ED structure stands out from the existing architecture so drivers can easily recognize it, and gives patients, families and hospital personnel quick access to waiting areas, 36 adult and 10 pediatric treatment spaces, trauma space, corridors, office and storage areas, employee health examination room and staff MD on-call rooms. Evidence-based design principles and a consistent focus on the patient have also produced an interior environment with generous daylight and views, lively color schemes representing the seasons and the earth, motifs drawn from nature such as the cylindrical bubble column in the pediatric waiting area, and playful, hospitality-inspired contemporary furnishings. Speaking for his colleagues, Dr. William Maloney, Condell's medical director of emergency services, has declared, "Our expanded emergency department will enable Condell to serve the region's needs well into the future as Lake County continues to grow."

Below and bottom: Exterior

Opposite top, left to right: Pediatric waiting, pediatric treatment, pediatric corridor intersection

Opposite bottom: Pediatric treatment corridor

Photography: Mark Ballogg © balloggphoto.com

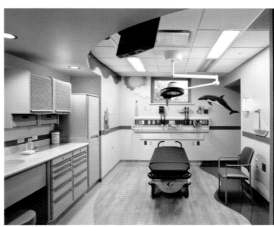

Anderson Mikos Architects, ltd.

Rush-Copley Medical Center
Connecting Entry Atrium and Lobby
Aurora, Illinois

Unprecedented demand for its services has prompted Rush-Copley Medical Center, a 183-bed general hospital in Aurora, Illinois, to add 26 medical-surgical inpatient beds, a second physician office building, a 500-vehicle parking structure, and a new main entrance, a connecting entry atrium and lobby that link the hospital and physician office buildings. The two-story-high, 3,885-square-foot atrium and lobby function—literally and symbolically—as Rush-Copley's new front door, designed by Anderson Mikos Architects as a signature space as well as a campus hub. The scheme carefully alternates between the monumental exterior, featuring a two-story-high colonnade and port cochere, and the heightened yet more intimate interior, where millwork dividers define small seating groups of hospitality-inspired furnishings to promote family privacy and interaction. Staging the construction was another challenge. From minimizing disruption of operations, providing safe patient access to existing buildings, and maintaining an aggressive schedule, to relocating utility lines, devising a foundation to overcome poor soil conditions, and stabilizing and reinforcing existing adjacent retaining wall structures, the project required close collaboration among project team members. Patients and visitors are gratefully unaware of this, however, as they enter a sunny atrium that glows like a jewel at night.

Far left: Exterior with porte cochere

Left: Small seating group

Opposite top, left to right: Evening view of exterior, entrance to atrium and lobby, reception desk

Photography: Mark Ballogg © balloggphoto.com

Anderson Mikos Architects, ltd.

Riverside Regional Medical Center
5 West Inpatient Oncology Center
Newport News, Virginia

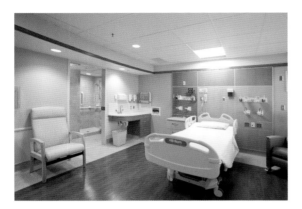

In a dramatic demonstration that one plus one can equal more than two, Riverside Regional Medical Center, in Newport News, Virginia, recently renovated the inpatient rooms for oncology and hemo/oncology at its 5 West Inpatient Oncology facility to create one shared unit with a warm, calming environment—in stark contrast to its predecessor. The one-floor, 14,500-square-foot facility, designed by Anderson Mikos Architects, combines two segregated, individually programmed departments, medical oncology and hemo/oncology, into a single holistic unit by introducing a centralized nurse station core to serve both units, a connection corridor that joins the units, and shared support spaces accessible from both units. To promote a new healing environment, the design transmits daylight deep inside the unit with transparent and translucent glass, provides space and accommodations for family members in patient rooms and public spaces, and establishes a hospitality-style ambiance through such carefully chosen materials as maple and cherry wood finishes, glass mosaic tile, stone-look porcelain tile, etched glass, quartz stone, solid surfacing, low-VOC paints and sophisticated lighting. In the midst of an extensive redesign program, 570-bed Riverside Regional Medical Center, which began serving the Virginia Peninsula in 1916, has updated its oncology facility with impressive, life-affirming results.

Above: Nurse station

Top left and upper left: Patient room

Left: Elevator lobby with café-style waiting area

Photography: John Warters/ Photo Reflections

Array Healthcare Facilities Solutions

Array Healthcare Facilities Solutions

St. Elizabeth Healthcare
Ambulatory Care Center and Emergency Department
Covington, Kentucky

Full-service, acute-care hospitals are indispensable to major population centers. However, local access is an important patient satisfaction element, as demonstrated by St. Elizabeth Healthcare's impressive new, three-floor, 120,000-square foot Ambulatory Care Center and Emergency Department, in Covington, Kentucky. Developed by Anchor Health Properties and designed by Array Healthcare Facilities Solutions as Architect of Record and Champlin Architecture as Associate Architect, the facility delivers the quality outpatient services (except surgery) Greater Cincinnati has trusted from St. Elizabeth since 1861. The contemporary building,

housing primary and specialty care, imaging, wound care, dialysis and laboratory services, features an emergency department as well. The facility is positioned prominently to emphasize its accessibility and designed to reflect community input. Accordingly, the healing experience begins once patients enter the site, where thoughtful campus planning is expressed through ease of parking, recognizable exterior wayfinding, healing gardens and direct access to appropriate entrances. After being greeted by facility personnel, patients follow a user-friendly wayfinding system anchored by a "Main Street" circulation corridor linking the central registration/lobby/

bistro area with all diagnostic imaging, dialysis and laboratory service sub-waiting areas as well as the emergency department with primary and specialty physicians. (Floors two and three house physician offices.) Hospitality inspired interiors complete the picture with comfortable furnishings, stone and wood finishes in public areas, rich colors and energy-conserving lighting that blends daylight with architectural lighting.

Right, top to bottom: Corridor, emergency care treatment room, emergency care nurse station, emergency care waiting

Below: Exterior at main entrance

Opposite: Main entrance/registration

Photography: Miles Wolf

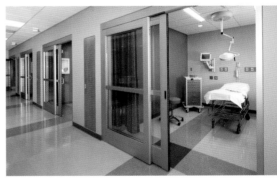

Array Healthcare Facilities Solutions
Payette Associates

Penn State Milton S. Hershey Medical Center
Cancer Institute
Hershey, Pennsylvania

The Penn State Milton S. Hershey Medical Center serves is the primary hospital for the Hershey community; it is also the medical school for Pennsylvania State University. As a teaching facility, the Center wanted the opportunity to bring cutting edge cancer research directly to their patient's bedside. As a community hospital, the Center wanted to offer a patient-focused healing environment. The new five-story, 180,000-square foot Cancer Institute, designed by Payette Associates as design architect and Array Healthcare Facilities Solutions as associate architect, successfully supports both goals. Clinical floors, with planning and design by Array, support radiation and medical and surgical oncology offering four linear accelerators, a 40-position infusion bay with views to a healing garden and other accommodations that provide state-of the-art cancer care in an environment designed to incorporate evidence-based design principles. Research floors, with planning and design by Payette, which also designed the exterior and public spaces, provide wet and dry laboratories and features breakout spaces and lounges to encourage informal meetings and collaboration. Physician offices and new entrance for the main Medical Center—a sunny, five-story atrium vertically connecting major circulation spaces—round out the distinctive program. The new Cancer Institute was sited to create a new public gateway that realigns the entire medical campus complex.

Above: Infusion bays
Right: Radiation waiting area
Below: Healing garden
Opposite top, left to right: Infusion nurse station, corridor, infusion room
Photography: Warren Jagger

Array Healthcare Facilities Solutions
Parkin Architects, Ltd.

University Hospitals, Rainbow Babies & Children's Hospital
Neonatal Intensive Care Unit
Cleveland, Ohio

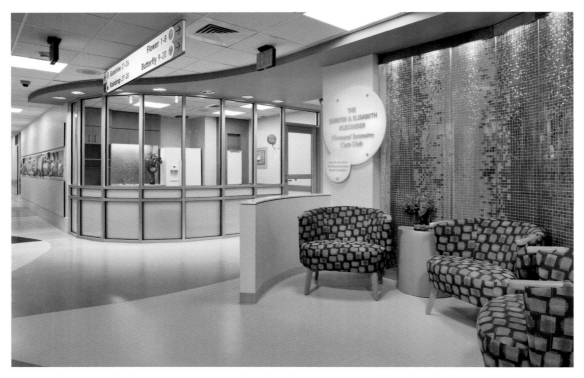

Left: NICU entrance
Below: Parent area within patient room
Bottom: Patient room
Opposite: Pedestrain bridge
Photography: Scott Pease

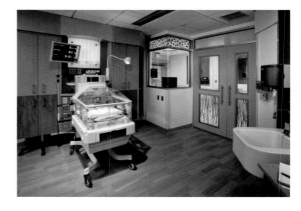

The former neonatal intensive care unit (NICU) at Rainbow Babies and Children's Hospital—part of Cleveland's University Hospitals and one of America's best children's hospitals as ranked by *U.S. News & World Report*—was undersized by current space benchmarks. The Hospital recognized the benefits of a single-room NICU model, but required a design that would not raise operating costs. Array was engaged to do preliminary test fit planning and provide interior design services with Parkin Architects as Architect of Record for a replacement Unit to address capacity demands as well as provide a model of care infused with the latest in evidence-based design and family-centered care. To accomplish this, the 38-bed, one floor, 30,000-square-foot Level III/IV NICU groups patient rooms into four pods that enhance sightlines and reduces footsteps for staff, letting clinicians deliver the high level of neonatal care for which Rainbow is renowned. Patient rooms provide privacy and space for families to bond with their infants, each offers a daybed, nursing recliner, breast pump and breast milk refrigeration, as well as individual lighting and sound controls. Family-focused features extend well beyond the patient room and

include a parent resource room, support and respite areas. To promote a soothing, hopeful experience for all families, Array developed a themed environment that would incorporate whimsical yet enduring elements. A series of visioning workshops culminated in the adoption of a rainbow theme that incorporates various elements of nature and reflects the Hospital's established brand identity. Butterfly, flower, sunshine and raindrop are the four pod names derived from the Rainbow theme, used as wayfinding icons, framed by the water ribbon flooring element which flows through each pod. To reinforce the nature-inspired theme, real plant materials such as flowers and grass are embedded in decorative glass and resin materials throughout the space. This theme and associated colors, forms and icons, serve as visual cues to families to navigate the Unit. Wood-look flooring, decorative cast glass, and nature-inspired colors and finishes, create an elegant and whimsical environment that evokes a child's world without being childish.

Left: Entrance to "Flower" pod
Above left: Nurse station
Above: Clinical work area

Ascension Group Architects

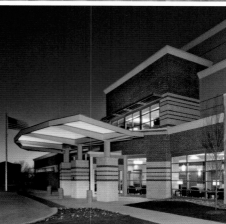

1250 East Copeland Road, Ste. 500 • Arlington, TX 76011 • 817.226.1917 • 817.226.1919 (Fax)

www.ascensiongroup.biz

Ascension Group Architects

Forest Park Medical Center
Dallas, Texas

Developing a full-service, acute-care hospital imposes many requirements, including an accessible site with room for expansion, as patients and visitors will discover at the new, two-story, 66,090-square-foot Forest Park Medical Center, in Dallas, designed by Ascension Group Architects. The proposed site, bordered by highway frontage and a winding creek, was separated from available expansion space by a high-voltage transmission easement. Ascension Group's planning studies resulted in the repositioning of the facility on an adjacent lot, accommodating growth now underway, and the construction of a medical office building on the proposed site, a project completed in July 2010. Inside the stucco, aluminum and glass-clad contemporary building, patient-friendly facilities include eight operating rooms, endoscopy room, 19-bay preoperative and postoperative area, imaging center with MRI, CT and R&F rooms, 24 inpatient beds, emergency department with four examination/triage rooms, respiratory therapy, dietary kitchen, dining spaces, and administrative suites. An atrium and public corridor provide easy access to these facilities, leading patients and families to interiors featuring comfortable, contemporary furnishings that include oversized seating for the region's bariatric patient population and such hospitality-inspired touches in patient rooms as wood-look flooring and warm colors. At night, lighting gives the hospital visual appeal from the highway.

Above: Lobby atrium

Left: Exterior detail

Right: Corridor

Opposite top left, center: Nursing department waiting, patient room

Opposite bottom: Exterior at night

Photography: Mark Trew

Ascension Group Architects

Baylor Orthopedic and Spine Hospital at Arlington
Arlington, Texas

A new, two-story, 57,242-square-foot Baylor Orthopedic and Spine Hospital of Arlington, in Arlington, Texas, designed by Ascension Group Architects, is responding to rapid population growth in the community by providing quality care for patients needing treatment for spine and orthopedic conditions. The joint effort of Baylor Health Care System, Arlington Orthopedic Associates and United Surgical Partners International, the brick, stucco, metal and glass-clad structure features a 24-bed inpatient surgery center, six large operating rooms, radiology suite, 24-hour emergency department with two examination/triage rooms, administrative offices and 24-hour food service. Its overall scheme will easily allow two operating rooms and 12 patient rooms to be added in the future without disturbing daily operations. Among its state-of-the-art features are spacious, 900-plus-square-foot ORs, designed not only to accommodate orthopedic surgeries, but also to support teaching programs for caregivers within the facility and on the Internet. The hospital is patient-friendly outside as well as inside. Because Baylor Healthcare System required it to be constructed near an existing medical office building and surgery center to maximize operational efficiencies, the new hospital is readily accessible via I-20 and North Matlock Road and is adjacent to several hotels, making it convenient for family members needing lodging.

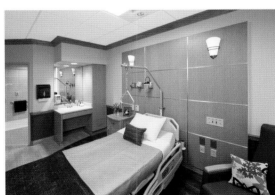

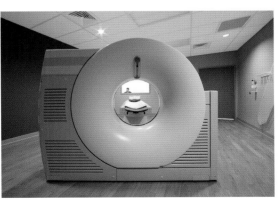

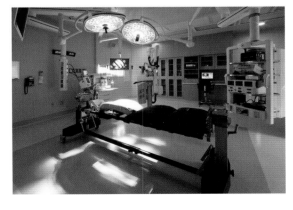

Ascension Group Architects

Texas Regional Medical Center at Sunnyvale
Sunnyvale, Texas

Residents of Rockwall, Hunt, east Dallas and west Kaufman counties in north Texas—a fast-growing area that is home to some 550,000 people—can now turn for their healthcare services to the new, 70-bed, two-story, 118,000-square-foot Texas Regional Medical Center at Sunnyvale, in Sunnyvale, Texas, a general, acute-care, for-profit hospital developed by Cottonwood Partners and Rockwall Hospitals Inc. and designed by Ascension Group Architects. The first hospital built in Sunnyvale, an upscale, community of some 4,000 residents 15 miles east of downtown Dallas, the Center incorporates 53 medical/surgical suites, six operating rooms, endoscopy room, catherization laboratory, eight-bed intensive care unit, emergency department with six treatment rooms, a Women's Center with labor-and-delivery suites, operating rooms for Caesarean sections, 10-bed nursery for newborns and postpartum rooms, pharmacy, laboratory, kitchen and materials management. Recognizing the importance of being first, the building shrewdly projects a low-key, contemporary image. With state-of-the art equipment and a well-trained staff of healthcare professionals working in a healing environment that is attractive, relaxed and comfortable, patients and their families can receive top quality medical services in a reassuring, small-town setting, capturing a critical moment in the history of a region that is rapidly being transformed by urbanization.

Above: Café

Below: Main lobby

Right: Exterior at main entrance

Opposite top left, right: Patient room, exterior of Women's Center

Photography: Gene Fichte

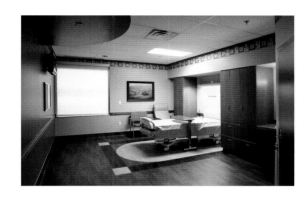

Ascension Group Architects

USMD Hospital
USMD Cancer Treatment Center
Arlington, Texas

To design the new, one-floor, 16,000-square-foot, state-of-the-art Urology Clinic and Cancer Treatment Center at USMD Hospital, in Arlington, Texas, Ascension Group Architects has so skillfully balanced the needs of hospital, staff and patients that the resulting spaces meet a wide range of objectives within what is apparently a seamlessly integrated environment. Not only does the Cancer Treatment Center incorporate the latest in medical technology, anticipate future technology, and establish a calming and aesthetically pleasing environment with optimal patient/staff flow, it gives the Center a separate identity while blending with the hospital, makes provisions for future expansion, keeps the Clinic distinct from the Center while integrating their facilities, and uses its limited square footage efficiently to fulfill an extensive program. Careful planning enables the design to include 15 examination rooms, procedure room, four patient consultation rooms, seven physicians' offices, physics and dosimetry, nurse stations, nurse work areas, phlebotomy, men's and women's sub-waiting rooms, staff offices and support spaces, one linear accelerator vault, one CT scan, and provisions for future additions, including a poured-in-place vault or modular vault within the facility's footprint. Notes Dr. Peter Lanasa, the Center's radiation oncologist, "The daily feedback received from patients has been outstanding!"

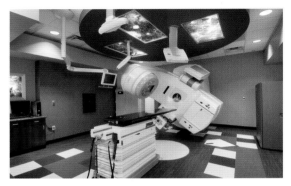

Top: Feature wall
Above: Linear accelerator
Below: Lobby/waiting area
Photography: Greg Kopriva

Cannon Design

2170 Whitehaven Road • Grand Island, NY 14072 • 716.774.3252 • 716.773.5909 (Fax)

www.cannondesign.com

Cannon Design

Stony Brook University Medical Center
Major Expansion Program
Stony Brook, New York

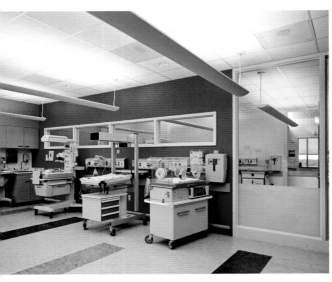

As Long Island's sole academic medical center and Suffolk County's only tertiary hospital and Level 1 Trauma Center, Stony Brook University Medical Center, in Stony Brook, New York, has been committed to excellence in patient care, research, education, and community service since 1980. Its recently completed expansion program allows it to consolidate and expand women's and children's services, triple the emergency department's capacity, and renovate and expand surgical services through a 150,000-square-foot renovation and 150,000-square-foot addition, designed by Cannon Design. Among its major features are 10 state-of-the-art surgery units, emergency services for 100,000 annual visits, a Women's and Infants' Center, featuring 48 ante-partum and post-partum beds, 10-bed LBR, obstetrics suite, and 50-bed Level 3 NICU, and a new hospital entrance. Interestingly, the new entrance plays a pivotal role by reorganizing the Center so patients can proceed directly to services from the new lobby rather than wander through the existing one-million-square-foot facility. The first healthcare project initiated under New York State's Executive Order 111, requiring new and substantial renovations of public buildings to achieve at least a 20 percent improvement in energy efficiency and meet the criteria for a LEED rating, Stony Brook anticipates LEED Silver certification.

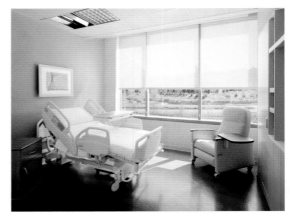

Top left: NICU
Top right: Lounge
Left: Exterior
Above: Patient room
Opposite: Entry lobby
Photography: Bjorg Magnea Photography

The directory sign reads:

Labor And Delivery
Elevator
Neonatal ICU
Parking Garage
Patient Tower Elevators
Cafeteria / Gift Shop
Admitting
Heart Center
Patient Discharge Lounge
Health Sciences Center
Chapel

Cannon Design

Advocate Lutheran General Hospital and Advocate Lutheran General Children's Hospital, Patient Care Tower
Park Ridge, Illinois

What are the advantages of a "non-mirrored" approach to patient room design? In the new, eight-story, 429,000-square-foot replacement patient tower at 645-bed Advocate Lutheran General Hospital, in Park Ridge, Illinois, patients have a direct route to the washroom, while the staff enjoys easy orientation and consistency for procedures in moving between patient rooms. It's one of many features that make the new patient tower, designed by Cannon Design, an effective healing environment for Advocate Lutheran, a top teaching, research and referral hospital serving Chicagoland. The new tower's extensive accommodations include a public lobby/reception, 15-bed PICU with family accommodations, 11-bed general pediatric unit, 4-bed intermediate care unit, 22-bed ICU, 10-bed interventional unit, three 34-bed nursing units,

28-bed mother-baby unit, and such amenities as a courtyard garden and rooftop terrace between new and existing buildings. Patient safety measures, floor plan efficiency and improved quality-of-life features for patients and caregivers contribute to its appeal. For example, each of the virtual "pods" on inpatient floors has a decentralized nursing station to decrease noise levels and travel distances, along with a column-free interior to improve sight lines and a universal floor plate that is easily convertible, acknowledging the likelihood of future change.

Above: Family accommodations

Left: Main entrance

Below: Nursing station

Below left: Exterior

Below far left: Public education center

Opposite: Public lobby/reception

Photography: Craig Dugan/Hedrich Blessing Photography and John Steinkamp Photography

Cannon Design

Brigham and Women's Hospital
Shapiro Cardiovascular Center
Boston, Massachusetts

Renowned for its innovative cardiovascular care, the Cardiovascular Center at Brigham and Women's Hospital, a 747-bed teaching affiliate of Harvard Medical School in Boston's Longwood medical area, has further enhanced its capabilities with the opening of the new, 10-story, 420,000-square-foot Shapiro Cardiovascular Center, designed by Cannon Design. Environments ranging from public spaces for everyday gatherings and special events to intimate areas offering warmth and comfort can be found among such state-of-the-art facilities as 16 operating suites, diagnostic and treatment facilities, 40 ICU rooms, 96 standard inpatient rooms, ambulatory care clinics, and public amenities that include dining facilities, conference rooms, family centers and consultation rooms. Facing the Hospital's main entrance across Francis Street, the Shapiro Center connects to it through two lower levels and a glass bridge spanning the street that feeds directly to the Hospital's main pedestrian street, the "Pike," facilitating the consolidation of cardiovascular services, improving the patient experience through operational efficiencies, and encouraging collaboration among specialists. Besides proclaiming the Hospital's continuing commitment to leadership in cardiovascular care, the Shapiro Center champions sustainability through LEED Silver certification—the first "green" building in the neighborhood.

Above: East lobby "pike" connection

Right: Bi plane endovascular room

Below: Perspective on Francis Street

Lower left: Stair along glass wall

Lower right: Patient room

Opposite: Exterior at night with glass bridge

Photography: Anton Grassl, Esto Photography

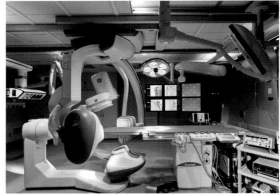

Cannon Design

The Lindner Center of HOPE
Comprehensive Behavioral Healthcare Center
Mason, Ohio

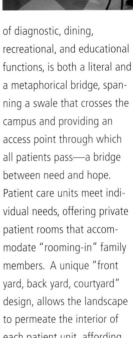

Situated on a 36-acre rolling meadow, the landscape for the state-of-the-art, free-standing behavioral healthcare Center, became the symbolic platform for understanding behavioral healthcare treatment, as well as a driving force in shaping the facility. In support of the "active treatment" model of care, the 64-bed facility is designed as a "treatment campus" utilizing the entire site to maximize patients' exposure to behavioral healthcare treatment. The Bridge Building, housing a "treatment mall" composed of diagnostic, dining, recreational, and educational functions, is both a literal and a metaphorical bridge, spanning a swale that crosses the campus and providing an access point through which all patients pass—a bridge between need and hope. Patient care units meet individual needs, offering private patient rooms that accommodate "rooming-in" family members. A unique "front yard, back yard, courtyard" design, allows the landscape to permeate the interior of each patient unit, affording every patient direct access to multiple landscapes—a connection to nature that creates a "grounding" effect for patients to monitor the passage of time, weather and seasonal changes. A symbolic point of arrival and departure, the lobby is a two-story glass enclosed space with views to the creek, bridge and woods. The dining room, with cathedral ceiling, features a stone fireplace that represents the warmth and comfort of home, enjoyable from either the outdoor terrace or dining room.

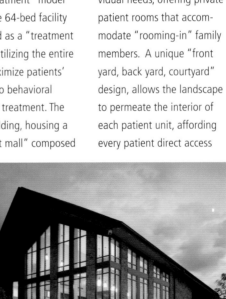

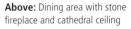

Above: Dining area with stone fireplace and cathedral ceiling

Left: Main lobby with two-story glass wall

Far left: Main entry at night

Lower left: Overall site plan

Photography: Tim Wilkes Photography

Christner, Inc.

7711 Bonhomme Avenue • St. Louis, MO 63105 • 314.725.2927 • 314.725.2928 (Fax)

www.christnerinc.com

Christner, Inc.

St. John's Mercy Medical Center
Heart and Vascular Hospital
St. Louis, Missouri

Every survivor of a cardiac episode is a lifetime heart patient. Accordingly, the new, nine-floor, 340,000-square-foot Heart and Vascular Hospital, on the 80-acre campus of St. John's Mercy Medical Center in St. Louis, is designed by Christner to provide a continuum of care that begins with the emergency department, a primary portal for heart patients, and ends with rehabilitation services that improve their long-term prognosis. The first facility of its kind in greater St. Louis, the design comprises 96 all-private patient rooms, diagnostic and procedural laboratories, physicians' offices, and five operating rooms for cardiac, thoracic and vascular surgery as well as the ED in an exceptional, patient-centered environment. Inpatient floors, for example, feature patient rooms with accommodations for families, nurse stations distributed in "pods," one nurse station per four patient rooms, dedicated family waiting areas, and corridors that separate patients from visitors and supplies. Equally prominent are the three-story main lobby, a circulation hub leading to cardiac services and doctors' offices, and inviting interiors combining cherry wood finishes, warm colors, comfortable furnishings and artwork. Proof of the hospital's success includes a 50 percent drop in staff turnover and a 60 percent increase in overall patient satisfaction rankings.

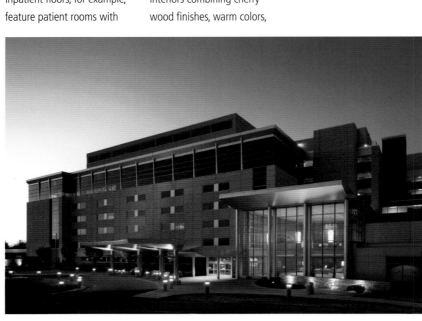

Clockwise, both pages, from top left: Waiting area in main lobby, OR, nurses station, patient room, main lobby, exterior

Photography: Debbie Franke; Christner, Inc.

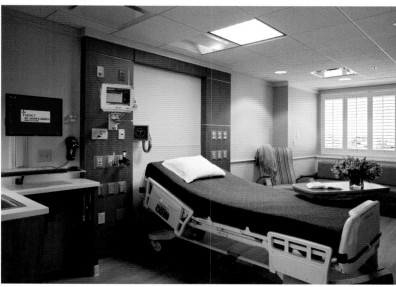

Christner, Inc.

St. John's Mercy Medical Center
Children's Hospital
St. Louis, Missouri

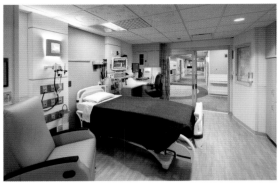

Designing a distinctive new Children's Hospital amidst the sprawling, 80-acre campus of St. John's Mercy Medical Center, in St. Louis, one of America's largest Catholic hospitals and the region's second largest hospital, presented Christner a challenge not unlike an intricate medical procedure. Not only did the firm's architects have to carve out space for a new, seven-floor, 360,000-square-foot patient tower, they established vertical and horizontal adjacencies with related services, including a new pediatric emergency department. The new tower consolidates inpatient pediatric services on three floors and establishes a marquee entry for the Children's Hospital while reserving space for future children's admitting and outpatient services. Two-thirds occupied by the 170-bed Children's Hospital, the new tower also inserts the final "puzzle piece" in the campus master plan to transform the 900-bed tertiary medical center into a more efficient, user-friendly campus, creating an interior pedestrian concourse that effectively links hospital services with parking, waiting, dining and information functions. Equally important, it gives patients, families and staff a supportive, state-of-the-art healing environment offering such features as patient rooms with designated family areas, distributed nurses' stations, each serving just six patient rooms, and nature-themed interiors that address the entire hospital population.

Clockwise, both pages, from left: Interior pedestrian concourse, corridor with directional singage and graphics, patient room, entrance lobby, nurses station

Photography: Sam Fentress

Christner, Inc.
SSM Cardinal Glennon Children's Medical Center
NICU and Surgery Addition
St. Louis, Missouri

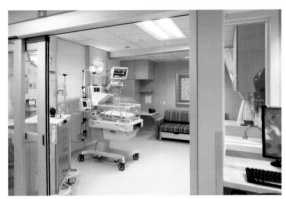

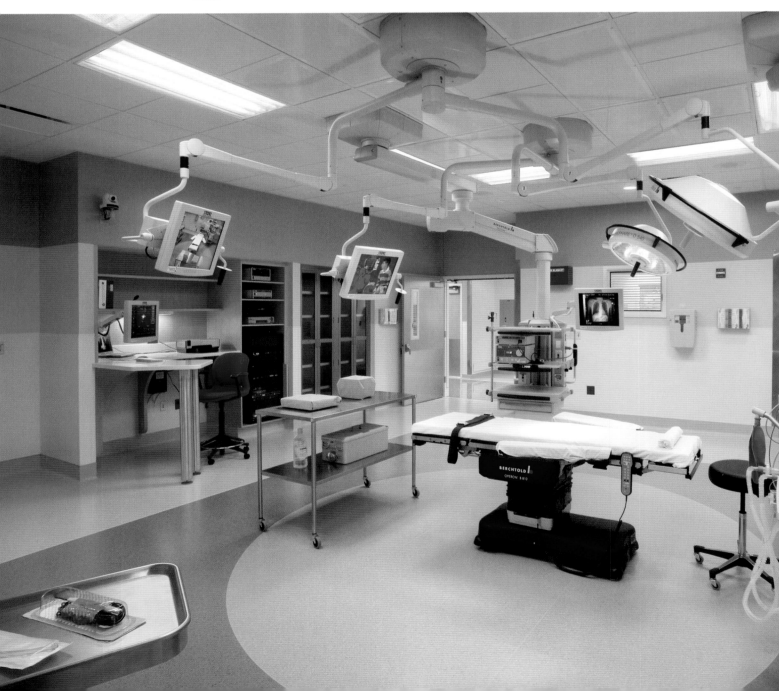

Clockwise, both pages, from far left: NICU patient corridor, patient room, NICU control desk, public entry and corridor, post-op recovery, operating room

Photography: Sam Fentress

The new, four-floor, 138,000-square-foot Neonatal Intensive Care Unit (NICU) and Surgery Addition adds much-needed new facilities to SSM Cardinal Glennon Children's Medical Center, the pediatric teaching hospital affiliated with St. Louis University School of Medicine that has served greater St. Louis for over 50 years: ten operating rooms, 60-bed NICU, new Central Sterile, and shell space for future relocation of

Radiology and Laboratory. Yet the award-winning project, designed by Christner, delivers more than capacity. First, the surgery suite provides a platform for new technology and flexibility for future change. Operating rooms equipped with leading edge technologies are designed identically to be used by any specialty, and can be reconfigured without demolition or construction to meet future needs. For the NICU, the care

model is built around all-private patient rooms without increasing staffing ratios from the former open-ward arrangement. Its innovative patient "pods," flanked by staff support areas and a family lounge, were developed in consultation with nurses, administrators and volunteer parents, replacing the central nurse station with dispersed stations and supplemental charting alcoves that permit direct

observation of patients, while maintaining the staff's vital sense of connectivity through electronic communications. Consequently, job satisfaction among staff members has reached 94 percent.

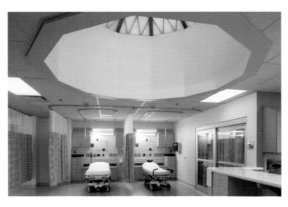

Christner, Inc.

SSM Cardinal Glennon Children's Medical Center
Warner's Corner
St. Louis, Missouri

Adolescent inpatients at SSM Cardinal Glennon Children's Medical Center, in St. Louis, the pediatric teaching hospital affiliated with St. Louis University School of Medicine, have never had a dedicated space like the new, one-floor, 1,000-square-foot Warner's Corner, designed by Christner. Respecting the complex nature of this age group, Cardinal Glennon and Christner have thoughtfully established a recreational retreat from the hospital's clinical environment that offers a comfortable and playful setting for different types of small group activity. The long, narrow space accommodates two lounges for movie and television viewing, a gameplay/group activity room and a computer room with Internet access. One area flows into another using curved walls and narrow openings to create acoustic buffers, while bright colors and low-scaled furniture make the small areas seem bigger. Since Cardinal Glennon and Kurt Warner's First Things First Foundation were determined to create a truly enjoyable experience for adolescents, the sophisticated A/V and computer technology in Warner's Corner is framed by a lively contemporary interior design employing high-end modern furnishings, bright, saturated colors, durable but attractive finishes, and sensitive lighting that features constantly changing LEDs at the dramatic entrance. One glance tells inpatients 11 and older, Warner's Corner is theirs.

Clockwise from bottom right: Computer room, gameplay/group activity room, movie and TV lounge, entrance

Photography: Sam Fentress

Earl Swensson Associates, Inc.

2100 West End Ave., Suite 1200 • Nashville, TN 37203 • 615.329.9445 • 615.329.9482 (Fax)

www.esarch.com

ESa

Atrium Medical Center
Middletown, Ohio

A new era began for Middletown Regional Hospital, founded in 1917 in Middletown, Ohio, when Atrium Medical Center opened as the centerpiece of the new, 190-acre Premier Health Campus. Cited by *U.S. News & World Report* as one of America's top hospitals, Middletown Regional faced major challenges to renovation and expansion on its 26-acre campus. Because

a new building on a site close to Interstate 75 and Route 122 was more cost effective and offered greater potential, ESa was retained to design Atrium Medical Center, a 279-bed, five-story, 544,443-square-foot replacement hospital. The relocation dramatically expands the scope and sophistication of services and establishes an outstanding patient- and family-centered environment.

Thus, besides providing state-of-the-art facilities for cardiac care, sports medicine, physical therapy, cancer program and women's services, Atrium offers warm, hospitality-inspired interiors that include all-private patient rooms with family space and sofa beds, family accommodations throughout the hospital, intuitive wayfinding and popular amenities. Better yet, Atrium now shares a campus

with such whole-life oriented neighbors as a children's specialty care center, senior residence and Atrium Family YMCA, housing Atrium's sports medicine, physical therapy and athletic training services alongside a childcare center, fitness facilities and community meeting space.

Above left: Main lobby

Above: Exterior at main entrance

Far left, left: Oncology/infusion, Professional Building lobby

Opposite bottom, left to right: MRI suite, lounge in Heart waiting

Photography: Jeff Millies and Scott McDonald © Hedrich Blessing

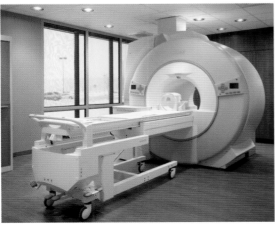

ESa

LeConte Medical Center
Sevierville, Tennessee

Located in the foothills of heavily visited Great Smoky Mountains National Park, LeConte Medical Center, in Sevierville, Tennessee, recently replaced aging and overcrowded Fort Sanders Sevier Medical Center, and experienced high patient volume in its emergency department—averaging 150 patients daily—from opening day. LeConte's busy ED isn't surprising, since its predecessor served four contiguous communities plus millions of tourists for 40-plus years. But the handsome new hospital, designed to evoke historic local architecture by ESa, design architect and interior designer, and Barber McMurray Architects,

architect of record, exceeds the former square footage while holding the bed count at 79 because of dramatic advances in treatment, technology and patient care services. The three-story, 200,000-square-foot structure shares its 70-acre campus with a 30,000-square-foot medical office building, 30,000-square foot Dolly Parton Center for Women's Services (named for its donor, the celebrated entertainer and Sevier County native), and 16,000-square-foot Cancer Center, all designed by the same architects, giving patients access to an unprecedented array of medical specialties and technologies. Impressive as these

capabilities are, patients and families also enjoy the healing environment that shelters them, featuring private patient rooms, daylight, scenic views and good wayfinding—which anyone near a national park can appreciate.

Above left: Health Unit Coordinator desk, LDRP

Left: LDRP

Below left: Exterior at main entrance

Below, bottom: Dining, ED trauma bay

Opposite: Main lobby

Photography: © Kyle Dreier Photography

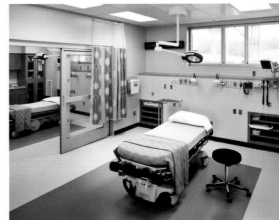

ESa

Midwest Medical Center
Galena, Illinois

It's fair to say people visiting the historic resort community of Galena, Illinois sought medical treatment at the former Galena-Stauss Hospital & Healthcare Center, a 45-year-old, 18-bed critical access facility, because they had to. Galena-Strauss's shortcomings were inescapable when the hospital chose to build anew rather than renovate and expand. The 25-bed, two-story, 94,082-square-foot replacement hospital, Midwest Medical Center, designed by ESa, features a main hospital tower and attached medical office building on a new, 35-acre site. While the hospital contains such facilities as the main lobby, admitting, diagnostics, physicians'

services, emergency department, ORs, laboratory, pharmacy, dining, gift shop and administration on the first floor, and 25 medical/surgical beds on the second floor, the MOB accommodates physical therapy/fitness, physicians' services and hospital information management services on the first floor, and shelled physicians' space on the second floor. Beyond fulfilling technical requirements, the design honors Galena's historic architecture through such detail as the clock tower, brick masonry and slate roof (simulated in fiberglass). As a Planetree affiliate (Illinois's first), the hospital also provides patient-centered, holistic care in a healing environment

incorporating residential and hospitality design concepts, starting with the main lobby's soaring, yet, soothing two-story space.

Top: Exterior at front entry

Above right, above far right: Nurses' station, fitness/rehabilition

Right, far right: Dining, patient room

Opposite: Main lobby

Photography: Jeff Millies and Craig Dugan © Hedrich Blessing

ESa

Vanderbilt University Medical Center
Critical Care Tower
Nashville, Tennessee

Patients admitted into hospitals today tend to be sicker than their predecessors, and the new 102-bed, 11-story, 329,000-square-foot Critical Care Tower at Vanderbilt University Medical Center, in Nashville, Tennessee, illustrates how teaching institutions are responding. The Critical Care Tower, designed by ESa, architect of record and interior designer, and Donald Blair & Partners, Architects, design architect, offers extensive facilities for advanced treatment and technology, including 12 interchangeable operating rooms and three of Vanderbilt University Hospital's intensive care units: surgical, neurological and medical. All facilities reflect leading-edge design. Each OR, for example, has three booms for lights, monitors, equipment and anesthesia as well as telemedicine capabilities, OR shelving standardized for restocking, and space for any equipment. Each patient room, private and averaging 320 square feet, is divided into staff, patient and family zones, with the patient zone featuring an ICU smart bed and headwall, and the family zone providing an active waiting area with television and computer as well as sleeper sofa or recliner. Purposeful as everything is, there is also an airy central atrium that visitors and staff can enter on the sixth floor, where a comfortable environment of lounge seating, live trees and artwork provides much-needed respite.

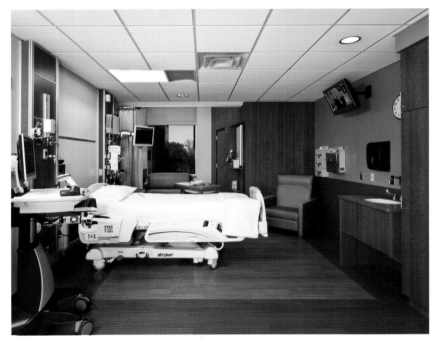

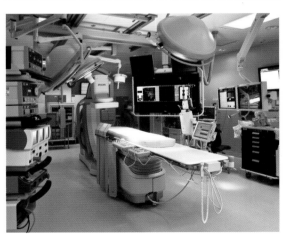

Above: Patient room
Top right: Central atrium
Center right: Patient floor

Bottom right: OR
Photography: ©Kyle Drier Photography

Ellerbe Becket, Inc., an AECOM Company

Ellerbe Becket, Inc., an AECOM Company

Stafford Hospital Center
Mary Washington Healthcare
Stafford, Virginia

The bold, contemporary form of the new, 100-bed, five-floor, 225,000-square-foot Stafford Hospital Center, designed by Ellerbe Becket, has transformed a 65-acre greenfield site adjacent to a wetland preserve bordering Stafford, Virginia's emerging downtown. Developed to serve a growing population, the acute care hospital addresses far-ranging concerns. The cruciform massing, for example, capitalizes on the site's topography to create distinct quadrants and serve as the organizing principle of building and landscape. The hospital clusters around the intersecting axes, positioning the main reception and visitor elevators at the center alongside a three-story atrium and curving glass curtainwall that anchors the east-west "main street," linking the medical procedure zone with nursing units, and offering amenities such as the chapel, dining, outdoor terrace and upper-level waiting areas. (The north-south entry axis connects the main campus entrance, reception and visitor parking.) Forward-looking and supportive, the design exemplifies the community-based non-profit Mary Washington Healthcare's brand. Outside, the architecture's material palette, including stone, brick, steel and glass, and human-scale design vocabulary acknowledge Stafford's rich history without mimicking it. Inside, attractive interiors, offering such features as full toilet rooms for critical care beds to reduce the risk of infection, introduce innovations supported by evidence-based design principles.

Left: Exterior

Right, top to bottom: Emergency department, main reception area, labor and delivery, nurses station

Opposite: Atrium

Photography: © Don Pearse

Ellerbe Becket, Inc., an AECOM Company

Park Nicollet Melrose Institute
St. Louis Park, Minnesota

The new, three-floor, 67,000-square-foot Park Nicollet Melrose Institute, located on a 3.5-acre site north of Park Nicollet Health Services' Park Center medical campus in St. Louis Park, Minnesota, is a unique facility serving patients seeking treatment for eating disorders. Designed by Ellerbe Becket, the project also includes a 136-car parking structure and healing garden. The facility supports Park Nicollet's newly developed treatment model with specially configured accommodations for group and one-on-one therapy in a school-like environment that celebrates Minnesota's climate, natural beauty and architectural vernacular. Floor plans are straightforward, since the award-winning structure was originally envisioned as a lease property. Thus, the first floor contains most semi public program elements, including the lobby atrium, family resource center, main dining room, fireplace lounge, chapel and bookstore, the second floor contains additional semi private program elements, including experiential kitchens and examination rooms, and the third floor contains inpatient and residential programs. While not a "lock-down" facility, the psychiatric treatment center promotes openness while discreetly discouraging patients from leaving and segregating some populations from others. The building is designed to accommodate future expansion, so that it may grow along with this important treatment program. Feedback from building users is testament to the project's success: families and staff declare "The Melrose Institute is the perfect setting for the treatment of eating disorders."

Clockwise, both pages from above: Non-denominational chapel, dining terrace, atrium, exterior at main entrance, examination room, welcome desk, solarium

Photography: © Don Wong

Ellerbe Becket, Inc., an AECOM Company

Group Health Cooperative Bellevue Medical Center
Bellevue, Washington

Profound change—in both operations and facilities—has revitalized Seattle-based Group Health Cooperative, serving over 600,000 residents of Washington and Idaho. Founded in 1947, Group Health is one of America's original healthcare cooperatives. While it provided full-service inpatient and outpatient care for decades, an aging facility, remote location and strong competition eroded its healthcare market share. In response, Group Health eliminated its inpatient program to focus on outpatient services, partnering with Overlake Regional Medical Center to provide inpatient care to its members. Group Health's new, four-floor, 189,000-square-foot outpatient facility, adjacent to Overlake Hospital in Bellevue, east of Seattle, lets Group Health's physicians practice in both facilities. The exceptionally flexible and efficient building, designed by Ellerbe Becket and NAC|Architecture, accommodates ever-changing technologies and treatments in a patient-centered environment. At its heart is the modular clinic. Here, all examination rooms are constructed on the same module with standard sinks and storage units to accept specialty carts parked in the same location in each room, always meeting current demand. Simultaneously, clustered workstations of medical assistants serve multiple examination rooms with greater productivity and less manpower. Group Health's Dr. Michael Erikson proudly observes, "Ellerbe Becket is an agent of change for Group Health Cooperative."

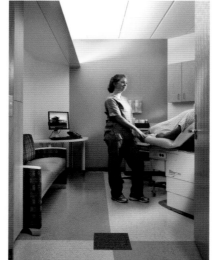

Clockwise from top: Primary exterior view with water feature, examination room, infusion bays, clinic module with multi-assignable medical assistants' workstations, main entrance

Opposite: Atrium lobby

Photography: Benjamin Benschneider

Ellerbe Becket, Inc., an AECOM Company

Samsung Medical Center
Samsung Cancer Center
Seoul, South Korea

Asia's largest cancer center, the new, 652-bed, 11-story (plus eight-level underground), 1.2-million-square-foot Samsung Cancer Center at Samsung Medical Center, in Seoul, South Korea, was designed by Ellerbe Becket in association with Samoo Architects + Engineers to combine treatment, research and education. The award-winning structure comprises four basic planning blocks: support podium/medical school, outpatient podium, inpatient tower and public atrium, providing a clear diagram for function and form with connections to existing facilities. Located in a conservation zone on a forested hillside that encircles the site, it limits above grade construction and plants green roofs to maximize green space, create healing gardens and control water runoff. Its flexible infrastructure and spatial modularity will accept future changes in cancer treatment while supporting state-of-the-art operations now. Yet it is also a thoughtful healing environment that enhances relationships between nature, patients, families and staff with user-friendly public and private spaces, accessible public areas that enjoy visual access to forest and gardens, and a clinical setting that is integrated with teaching and education facilities to break down barriers between teachers, staff and patients. For an institution that aspires to be Asia's medical hub of cancer treatment, the Cancer Center records an impressive milestone.

Above left and right: Healing garden, public atrium

Right: Exterior view of cancer center from roof garden

Photography: Seung Hoon Yum

EwingCole

100 North 6th Street • Philadelphia, PA 19106 • 215.625.4119 • 215.574.0952 (Fax)

www.ewingcole.com

EwingCole

Cooper University Hospital Pavilion
Camden, New Jersey

Patients and visitors gaze in wonder and delight as they enter the soaring, three-story, bamboo-filled lobby at the new patient care Pavilion of Cooper University Hospital, in Camden, New Jersey, where a cascade of natural light welcomes them to a reception desk, restaurant, health resource center, business center, gift shop, coffee shop and chapel. At the same time, staff members in the Pavilion's clinical laboratory do not experience the sense of confinement normally associated with a basement location, thanks to a design that combines natural light captured by transom windows with sophisticated electric lighting, ceiling coves and interior glass. This user-friendly facility is clearly no accident. As the clinical campus of the University of Medicine and Dentistry/ Robert Wood Johnson Medical School, Cooper University Hospital is a 540-bed institution dedicated to medical education and research excellence as well as the comprehensive medical care it has provided to residents of southern New Jersey since 1887. The 10-story, 370,000-square-foot Pavilion, designed by EwingCole, houses 12

operating room suites, 60 private medical/surgical rooms, 30-bed intensive care unit, and 12,000-square-foot addition to the emergency department, in addition to the laboratory and public lobby, in a setting where health care spaces are anchored by public spaces that extend the spatial feel of the hospitality-inspired lobby. Patients and families instantly appreciate the details in such facilities as the all-private medical/surgical patient rooms, which follow the innovative Planetree philosopy in offering patients choices and control over many aspects of their care. At approximately 305 square feet, for example, each room features a bed angled to give the patient a better view outside and the nurse a clearer view of the bed from the doorway, ample space for family members, and stylish yet comfortable furnishings. In addition, headwall outlets are positioned on the side of the bed, so staff members do not reach over patients

Above right: Exterior

Right: Reception desk in public lobby

Opposite: Public Lobby

Photography: Barry Halkin, Eduard Huber

EwingCole

to use medical devices and family members do not see a battery of equipment directly over the patient's head. The caregiver hand washing sink is located in an alcove just inside the room, satisfying clinical requirements while reducing the room's clinical appearance. Summing up public and professional praise for the design, John P. Sheridan, Jr., the Hospital's president and CEO, has commented, "The attention to detail is what sets the Pavilion apart from other area facilities. When you enter the facility, it gives you the sense you're in a healing environment."

Right: Family lounge
Below: Patient room
Opposite: Medical/surgical corridor

EwingCole

AtlantiCare
Oncology Center
Egg Harbor Township, New Jersey

Right: Core wall in main lobby
Below: Exterior
Opposite: Main lobby and stair
Photography: Barry Halkin

Taking advantage of the life-affirming correlation between nature and healing, AtlantiCare has developed a new outpatient cancer oncology center, AtlantiCare Cancer Care Institute, in Egg Harbor Township, New Jersey, that surrounds patients and

staff in a airy, uplifting and non-clinical environment. The two-floor, 39,600-square-foot structure, designed by EwingCole, organizes its facilities—comprising radiation oncology, which includes two linear accelerators, one cyberknife SRS system, and dedicated clinical, support and waiting space; medical oncology, which includes eight private infusion bays, one "buddy bay" with four stations, pharmacy, clinical support and dedicated waiting; diagnostic imaging, which includes one 64-slice PET/CT, one CT simulator, and shell space for an MRI, and physician lease space, conferencing/education areas, and a Gilda's Club cancer care support space—around an open, two-story spine that runs through the heart of the structure.

This natural view corridor, which focuses on the site's wooded areas and private gardens, works with indoor planters supporting bamboo tree stands, over 70 original works of art and extensive glazing on the perimeter to establish a direct visual link with the outdoors and bring natural light deep inside the building core. It is part of a coordinated effort to put state-of-the-art cancer care and medical technology at the service of patients and caregivers. Programmatic elements and departments,

for example, are arranged to eliminate operational inefficiencies and facilitate optimal clinical processes, while evidence-based design concepts are incorporated to help reduce medical errors, improve patient safety and ensure privacy, and design elements act as departmental identifiers, wayfinding aids and visual motifs that contribute to a sense of internal community. Conceived as a sustainable project and subsequently awarded LEED Gold Certification, the Institute has even inspired a proud staff to adopt work processes that further reduce waste and decrease energy and water usage within this outstanding environment.

Top: Infusion bay
Left: Medical oncology waiting
Above: Clinical support

FORMA Design

1524 U Street, NW • Suite 200 • Washington, D.C. 20009 • 202.265.2625 • 202.265.9588 (Fax)

www.FORMAonline.com

FORMA Design

Jill Bruno Orthodontics
Chevy Chase, Maryland

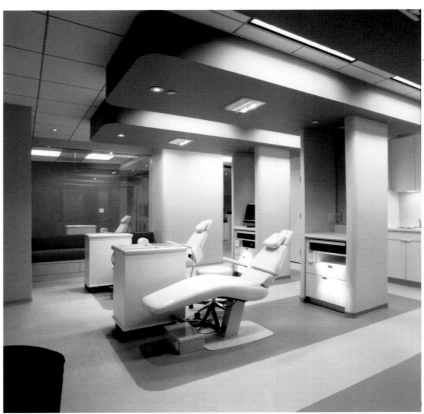

Most dental offices are filled with identical, compartmentalized spaces that patients scarcely notice or enjoy, but Dr. Jill Bruno, DMD, MSEd, was determined to avoid this stereotype. Working closely with FORMA Design, she developed a one-floor, 1,500-square-foot, 12th-story office in Chevy Chase, Maryland that expresses her dynamic, modern personality in an unusually open and highly comfortable setting. Spacious and uncluttered despite its numerous functions and modest square footage, Jill Bruno Orthodontics defines specialized facilities such as the treatment areas without isolating them by using cloud-like dropped ceilings, accent colors and glass partitions that frame views into other spaces, reinforces the sense of transparency by enclosing perimeter offices in glass walls, and streamlines workflow by locating the sterilization area in a niche off the corridor rather than a separate room. To evoke the touch of femininity Dr. Bruno desired, the architecture employs soft curves and rounded elements that appear to float in a neutral white shell animated by selected areas of color. "I wanted to appeal to an upscale patient base and a wide range of ages, from toddlers to adults," Dr. Bruno explains, adding that she and her patients are very pleased with FORMA's creative, award-winning design.

Above left: Reception desk and perimeter offices

Above: Open bay

Right: Corridor

Bottom right: View from consultation office to open bay

Opposite: Lobby seating

Photography: Geoffrey Hodgdon

FORMA Design

Mid-Atlantic Skin Surgery Institute
Waldorf, Maryland

As a new practice, the Mid-Atlantic Skin Surgery Institute, in Waldorf, Maryland, exploits the opportunity to start with a blank slate by creating a cutting-edge yet accessible office, tailored to the needs of the medical staff and patients drawn from suburban Washington, D.C. and the urban center itself. "My wife and I were searching for something different for our new dermatology office, something new and contemporary," recalls Institute leader Dr. George Verghese. "I needed a space which would create an inviting and tranquil environment for our patients." The one-floor, 5,000-square-foot modern facility, housing a practice that provides MOHS surgery and dermatological care as well as cosmetic procedures, meets his goal with such features as high ceilings, sculptural bulkheads, clear and sandblasted glass walls, all-white finishes accented with splashes of color, and a waterfall at the entrance. Perhaps its most distinctive feature is the glass-enclosed laboratory/staff core that straddles the front and rear perimeter corridors at the heart of the sunny, outward-looking facility. Not only does it promote access to and monitoring of laboratory functions from each operatory, it visualizes the laboratory-intensive nature of skin cancer surgery. Concludes Dr. Verghese, "We absolutely love working in our new office."

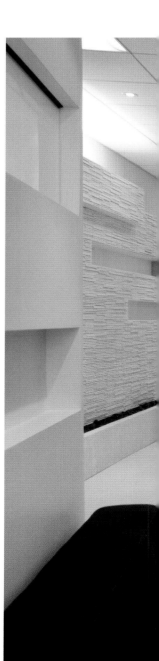

Left: Private office

Top: Corridor

Above: Laboratory/staff core

Opposite top left: Entrance

Opposite top right: Reception desk

Opposite: Reception

Photography: Geoffrey Hodgdon

FORMA Design   Obeid Dental
Chevy Chase, Maryland

A street-level corner location in a high-rise office building on busy Connecticut Avenue, in Chevy Chase, Maryland, has become a 1,600-square-foot prosthodontics office with a compelling public image for Dr. Youssef Obeid, DDS. Reflecting Dr. Obeid's young, progressive practice, the facility designed by FORMA Design features paperless, all-digital technology, unprecedented daylight and openness, and sophisticated architecture characterized by precision and detail—much like Dr. Obeid's

practice. The design functions well day and night. By day, the award-winning office is illuminated by daylight and outdoor views that make it cheerful and soothing for patients. By night, the sleek surfaces, rough stone wall and sophisticated lighting depict the space almost as a cool, club-like, go-to spot so photogenic that CNN immediately approached Dr. Obeid for an interview. More important, however, is the design's operational effectiveness. "FORMA helped me create a complete brand

identity for my practice," Dr. Obeid reports. "They provided a single source for everything, from the planning and the architecture to the logo, the graphics, the Website, the signage, the furnishings throughout, down to the accessories. They really understood what I wanted to achieve and worked with me to make it a reality. The response to the space has been fantastic."

Clockwise from top right:
Operatory, reception desk and work room, waiting area, view from street

Opposite: Reception and main corridor

Photography: Geoffrey Hodgdon

86

FORMA Design   Price Medical
Washington, D.C.

Patients needn't know that the new, one-floor, 3,800-square-foot office of Price Medical, located south of Dupont Circle in Washington, D.C., incorporates the demising walls of former studio apartments, because these immovable structures are seamlessly integrated as basic organizing elements. Price Medical, designed by FORMA Design, handles other existing conditions with similar creativity, using the reception area to split the space into a private doctor's suite to the left and the main part of the practice to the right. What matters more to Dr. Tim Price and his

staff, however, is that the peaceful, residential-style environment diminishes patients' stress. Their personal attention to patients is expressed through state-of-the-art equipment housed in a transparent, contemporary architecture of glass partitions, fine finishes and handsome detailing. The diagonal corridor, for example, widens towards the employee lounge at the end, accommodating a pre-function area outside the doctor's private office for meeting staff or patients, while glass partitions and light-filtering shades bring daylight indoors. In appraising a facility that

also includes private offices, patient consultation rooms, laboratory and blood-work rooms, examination rooms, and restrooms, Dr. Price declares, "Our patient rolls are full and the office is working and wearing well after four years."

Top: Examination room

Top center: Patient consultation

Above: Doctor's office

Left: Reception area

Photography: Geoffrey Hodgdon

Francis Cauffman

New York • Philadelphia • Baltimore

www.franciscauffman.com

Francis Cauffman

Morristown Memorial Hospital
Gagnon Cardiovascular Institute
Morristown, New Jersey

Renowned for its cardiac services, Gagnon Cardiovascular Institute at Morristown Memorial Hospital performs more heart surgery than any other hospital in the Garden State. As part of its plan to thoroughly improve its cardiology program, the hospital has developed a new, award-winning, five-floor, 206,000-square-foot facility designed by Francis Cauffman. The new construction saves money and increases effectiveness thanks to an innovative design scheme that expands the existing hospital vertically, avoiding the off-campus project initially planned. Designed to meet Gagnon's specific needs, the building features four cardiac ORs, four endovascular ORs, 88 cardiac care beds, 10 cardiac ICU beds, eight critical care beds, 14 cardiac PACU beds, outpatient facilities and two-story atrium with café and gift shop. Francis Cauffman's design emphasizes flexibility and the accommodation of long-term change: not only can the structural frame and foundation accommodate two additional floors, but cardiac patient rooms are adaptable to other services, and ORs feature strengthened framing and overhead floor slabs to meet the stringent vibration limits of sensitive neuro-surgery equipment. The new facility's impact has been dramatic; patient satisfaction has risen to 89 percent, putting Morristown Memorial Hospital in the top 5th percentile nationally.

Associate Architect: Buckl Architects

Above left and right: Lobby/ atrium, exterior

Right, far right: OR, lobby/ atrium in evening view

Opposite: Family waiting

Photography: Barry Halkin/ Halkin Photography, LLC

Francis Cauffman   Geisinger Wyoming Valley Medical Center
Critical Care Building
Wilkes-Barre, Pennsylvania

Geisinger Health System annually serves 2.6 million residents across central and northeastern Pennsylvania. 242-bed Geisinger Wyoming Valley Medical Center, in Wilkes-Barre, Pennsylvania, plays a major role within that network. Besides operating the region's only freestanding heart hospital, the Wilkes-Barre facility maintains a high-end cancer center, one of eight accredited chest pain centers in the state, and Luzerne County's only trauma center. Now, a new five-story, 178,000-square-foot Critical Care Building, designed by Francis Cauffman, introduces state-of-the-art space for emergency and surgical services. The brick-, metal- and glass-clad structure brings new vitality to the east end of the campus. Inside, a classic vertical stack of narrow patient unit floors, set above a wider emergency department and wider surgery floors, features 12 high-tech surgical suites, a 24-bed intensive care unit, 32-bed ED, and Level II trauma program. Granted LEED Silver certification, the award-winning design ushers in a new era of patient-centered care with comfortable furnishings, contemporary colors and textures, and spacious, daylight-filled patient rooms overlooking the surrounding mountains. Wayfinding features public circulation along the perimeter. Geisinger Health System's Lissa Bryan-Smith concludes, "Whereas the original buildings on campus were built for the health system, our recent buildings are built for its people."

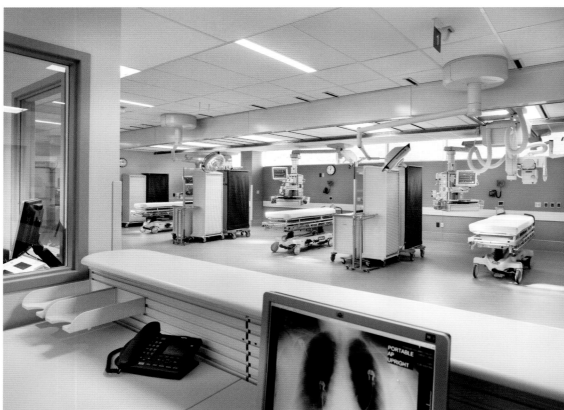

92

Far left, center left, left: Curtainwall detail, pre-surgery, exterior with public corridor

Below: Exterior at ED entrance

Opposite center, bottom left: ICUs, post-surgery

Photography: Barry Halkin/ Halkin Photography, LLC

Francis Cauffman

AtlantiCare Regional Medical Center
New Bed Tower and Renovation
Atlantic City, New Jersey

In developing its new, seven-story, 204,570-square-foot George F. Lynn Harmony Pavilion, AtlantiCare Regional Medical Center prioritized improvements in patient recovery, staff performance and operational safety. The interior design by Francis Cauffman incorporates principles of evidence-based design. The bed tower houses a 26-bed intensive care unit, two 30-bed (all private) medical/surgical floors, emergency department with dedicated diagnostic imaging suite, radiology department, and two floors for future medical/surgical private patient rooms. Its interiors promote healing and reduce stress by giving patients and families more control over their space. Clear wayfinding, supporting families as caregivers through zones in patient rooms, family waiting rooms and other family-oriented spaces, and providing access to nature through "positive distractions," including artwork, water feature, fireplaces in family waiting rooms, and patient education center with outdoor views. Every detail contributes to healing. Furniture, for example, uses clean lines, generous scale, rich upholstery and comfortable contours to welcome patients and families to relax. Full-spectrum color schemes stimulate as well as soothe. Founded in 1898 as Atlantic City's first hospital, AtlantiCare is prepared for 21st-century patients at its Harmony Pavilion.

Architect: Stantec

Top: Medical/surgical floor reception
Above: Patient room
Left: Family waiting room
Photography: Barry Halkin/ Halkin Photography, LLC

Francis Cauffman

Geisinger Wyoming Valley Medical Center
Henry Cancer Center
Wilkes-Barre, Pennsylvania

Long hours spent by cancer patients in chemotherapy have been thoughtfully anticipated at the new three-story, 39,000-square-foot addition to the Henry Cancer Center of Geisinger Wyoming Valley Medical Center, in Wilkes-Barre, Pennsylvania. The new outpatient building, designed by Francis Cauffman, creates an airy and inviting 24-treatment bay infusion area that supports either mingling with other patients (as is preferred at Geisinger) or taking solace in privacy. To accomplish this, the space employs a modular casework system with low-rise partitions framing interior glass, visual access to daylight and outdoor views, and clean, fresh colors that reference nature and the local region. The LEED-NC Certified structure also exploits its sloping site by positioning the main entrance in a curving wall on the high side of the slope. This configuration gives patients, who may be experiencing fatigue, depression or anxiety, a private drop-off that conveys them directly to the infusion area. Infusion patients face the building's second curving wall, and the healing garden it encircles; twenty examination rooms and physicians' offices fill most of the remaining space. The sophistication, clarity and sensitivity of the design help demonstrate why residents of central and northeastern Pennsylvania have trusted Geisinger for their health care since 1915.

Top left: Family lounge

Top right: Exterior showing main entrance and private drop-off

Above: Infusion area

Photography: Barry Halkin/ Halkin Photography, LLC

Francis Cauffman   St. Joseph's Regional Medical Center
New Critical Care Building
Paterson, New Jersey

Opened in 1867 by the Sisters of Charity of Saint Elizabeth, St. Joseph's Hospital, in Paterson, New Jersey, started operations with a modest 12-bed ward. Over 140 years later, St. Joseph's Healthcare System treats over 1.6 million patients annually at facilities that include St. Joseph's Regional Medical Center and St. Joseph's Children's Hospital on the Paterson campus. Facing rising demand for services, St. Joseph's has expanded and renovated facilities for years. A four-story, 171,000-square-foot Critical Care Building, designed by Francis Cauffman, will dramatically expand and upgrade the Center's capabilities. Its new adult and pediatric emergency departments, surgical suites, pre-operative and post-operative areas, four critical care units, rooftop helistop, and lobby with educational conference facilities, simultaneously reflect evolving patient needs and advances in treatment and technology. Among the building's many innovative features are a patient-focused environment that is modern, hospitality-inspired and easily navigated, and elliptically-shaped ICU pods that enhance staff's visual monitoring and reduce travel distances. A streamlined ED patient sequence should shorten wait times and direct exiting patients to check-out. The pediatric ED is meant for children—and shows it.

HDR Architecture, Inc.

8404 Indian Hills Drive • Omaha, NE 68114 • 800-366-4411 • 402.399.1282 (Fax)

www.hdrarchitecture.com

HDR Architecture, Inc.

Cleveland Clinic Abu Dhabi Hospital
Abu Dhabi, United Arab Emirates

Far left: VIP suite

Left: Gallery

Below: The Canyon

Opposite, upper left: Exterior, evening view

Opposite, upper right: Diagnostics and treatment

Opposite, lower right: Exterior, river view

Photography: Courtesy of HDR Architecture, Inc.

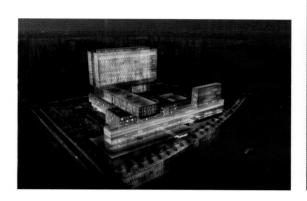

Cleveland Clinic Abu Dhabi Hospital, in the United Arab Emirates, is designed by HDR Architecture to be unlike any other hospital in the region. When completed, the 360-bed, 20-floor, three million-square-foot facility will attract patients worldwide, much as its U.S. counterpart does now. Consequently, the project resolves numerous unique challenges. Verticality is used imaginatively, for example, to create efficient through-put and minimize travel distances, stacking 18 floors of acute care patient rooms atop an orthogonal block of ICUs. These floors are perpendicular to patient room floors above and interventional surgical floors below. The ED stands just beneath the interventional surgical platform to directly transport critical ED patients to surgery. Color and universal sights and sounds provide cues to the project's innovative multinational wayfinding. To integrate Abu Dhabi's culture, the design incorporates such features as patient rooms for longer stays. These feature hotel-like environments with spaciousness and modern, elegant and comfortable furnishings where families can help patients heal, while observing such cultural norms as the separation of male and female patients. In addition, the design includes four 7,000-square-foot Royal Patient Suites in a rooftop penthouse, accommodating family, security and meetings, as well as clinical and operational activities, and sustainability features worthy of LEED Gold certification.

HDR Architecture, Inc.

University of South Florida Health
Byrd Alzheimer's Institute
Tampa, Florida

Above: Reception and waiting
Right: Staff dining
Below: Lobby
Below right: Curtainwall detail
Opposite: Exterior at main entrance
Photography: George Cott/ Chroma Inc.

The University of South Florida Health Byrd Alzheimer's Institute in Tampa was established in 2002 by the Florida Legislature under Speaker of the House Johnnie Byrd, whose father suffered from the disease. The staff of this translational research facility is dedicated to the prevention, treatment and cure of Alzheimer's and related disorders. The six-story, 108,000-square-foot facility, designed by HDR Architecture, provides the Institute a state-of-the-art patient clinic with integral imaging and evaluation areas, educational and conference space, data storage center, vivarium, office components and research laboratories for eight scientific teams. Its luminous spaces fulfill two dissimilar missions.

For patients, clinical areas employ flexible modules that provide a calming and soothing environment to support Alzheimer's care. In the laboratories, an open approach reduces potential for major modifications when scientific breakthroughs occur and/ or the facility's mission changes. What visitors may not discern, of course, is the facility's complex structural features, which result from the site's poor subsoil conditions and proximity to university freshwater supply wells. Occupants and visitors like what they see, as indicated by Dr. Huntington Potter, director, Florida Alzheimer's Disease Research Center, who declares, "This is the best designed translational research building I've ever seen."

HDR Architecture, Inc.

Reid Hospital and Health Care Services
Richmond, Indiana

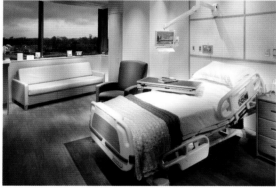

Above: Main Street corridor

Above right: Patient room

Top right: Lobby atrium seating

Right: Main lobby atrium

Far right: Exterior

Opposite upper right: Bridge entrance to campus

Photography: Jeffrey Jacobs Photography Inc.

Nearly a century after Reid Memorial Hospital opened in 1905 in Richmond, Indiana, the most cost-effective option for its future was building a new facility. The resulting 238-bed, six-story, 544,000-square-foot replacement hospital and three-story, 74,000-square-foot medical office building were designed by HDR Architecture. The projects not only relocate Reid Hospital but let this regional referral medical center offer east central Indiana and west central Ohio state-of-the-art medical treatment and technology within an exceptional healing environment. Featured are such advanced facilities as the Outpatient Care Center with self-registration kiosks, the comprehensive Heart Center connected to inpatient services with on-site cardiovascular surgeons, and the Mother-Baby Care Center with infant protection system. Patients discover all-private rooms and showers, quiet Critical Care rooms that accommodate family members, and such amenities as a café, espresso bar, gift shop, art program, patient-room computers, and fold-out sofas and card tables. Though most outpatient care is provided by joint-venture entities between Reid and its physicians, required separations between certain departments are not obvious to the public. For this and other reasons, Jon Ford, Reid Governing Board Chairman, declares, "The new Reid provides a beautiful healthcare campus that will allow our team to offer top-notch care using the latest technology."

HDR Architecture, Inc.

Renown Regional Medical Center
Reno, Nevada

The roots of Renown Regional Medical Center, in Reno, Nevada, trace back to the 1862 founding of Washoe Clinic. Here victims of a smallpox outbreak were treated amidst the turmoil of the Civil War and the Comstock Lode silver boom in nearby Virginia City.

Today's Center represents the modern heart of northern Nevada's largest and only locally owned, not-for-profit, integrated health network. The Center strives diligently to maintain its leadership, as evidenced by such state-of-the-art facilities as its Level II Trauma Center, Chest Pain

Center and Comprehensive Stroke Center. Its new 190-bed, 11-story, 512,000-square-foot bed tower has been designed by HDR Architecture to offer the guest experience of a high-end hotel. Private rooms, featuring stylish furnishings, private baths and spaces

for visitors, occupy patient floors where common areas are clustered around main lobbies to separate public and staff/patient areas and to simplify wayfinding. The concrete, metal panel- and glass-clad structure, which also houses expanded surgical services, imaging,

cardiology, emergency rooms and ICU beds, even is a welcoming landmark. Its concrete base is accentuated with a backlit translucent strip that admits natural light during the day and sends a dramatic ribbon of light across the desert at night.

Above: Exterior at main entrance
Right: Main lobby
Top left: Patient room
Top right: Emergency Department
Photography: © VanceFox.com

Health Facilities Group, LLC

142 N. Mosley, Suite 300 • Wichita, KS 67202 • 316.262.2500 • 316.264.2300 (Fax)

www.healthfacilitiesgroup.com

Health Facilities Group, LLC

Kiowa County Memorial Hospital
Greensburg, Kansas

Hospitals play major supporting roles during natural disasters, but when a tornado destroyed most of Greensburg, Kansas on May 4, 2007, it did not spare Kiowa County Memorial Hospital. Operating from tents, trailers, and modular buildings, the hospital's staff went back to work immediately, treating over 200 patients in the ER tent in the first month after the tornado. Now, a new replacement critical access hospital has opened, providing patient-focused facilities that fulfill the community's commitment to create a sustainable environment. The 15-bed, one-story (plus basement), 51,000-square-foot contemporary structure, designed by Health Facilities Group, houses existing and new services within its pre-cast concrete and glass exterior, including a five-provider clinic, specialty clinic, emergency department, radiology department, physical/occupational therapy department, laboratory and on-site daycare. To obtain LEED Platinum certification, it employs a wind turbine generator, gray water and rainwater systems, highly efficient HVAC system, locally sourced and recycled building materials, extensive daylighting and energy-conserving lighting featuring LED lamps and fixtures. Yet its cheerful, daylight-filled interiors, organized around a clerestoried spine wall corridor for easy wayfinding and appointed in durable furnishings that display modern flair, also quickly orient patients to the new location—directly across the street from the temporary hospital.

Above, in descending order: Nurses station, patient room, aerial view with windmill

Left: Exterior at main entrance

Opposite: Reception lobby

Photography: Steve Rasmussen

Health Facilities Group, LLC

Wilson Medical Center
Neodesha, Kansas

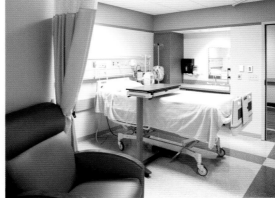

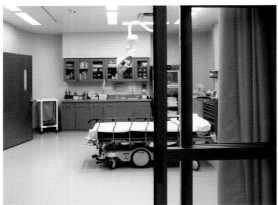

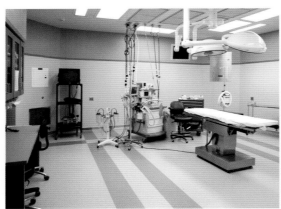

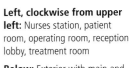

Left, clockwise from upper left: Nurses station, patient room, operating room, reception lobby, treatment room

Below: Exterior with main and emergency department entrances

Photography: Steve Swalwell/ Architectural Fotographics

Founded in 1913 as a county hospital in Neodesha, a rural community in southeast Kansas, Wilson Medical Center is a not-for-profit critical access hospital that continues to evolve in response to its patient population as well as medical treatment and technology. Its new, 15-bed, one-story, 46.000-square-foot replacement hospital, designed by Health Facilities Group, reveals how a high-quality healing environment can be developed despite a tight budget through creative design, careful selection of materials, and diligent project management. Noted for its unique Center for Wound Care and Hyperbaric Medicine, the new hospital additionally includes 15 private patient rooms, emergency department, expanded laboratory and imaging service departments, major and minor surgical and recovery suite, inpatient physical therapy, respiratory therapy and pain management clinic. (Outpatient clinical services, cardiac, podiatry, surgical, urology, and enhanced external counter pulsation are provided in the outpatient clinic area located in the medical office building adjacent to the hospital.) Mission-style furnishings give the interiors an informal, handsome and reassuring air appropriate to an institution nearly a century old. Delighted with the design, Deanna Pittman, the Center's administrator, recently observed, "They listened to us. They didn't go out and build what looks like every hospital in the state."

Health Facilities Group, LLC

Arbuckle Memorial Hospital
Sulphur, Oklahoma

Residents of Oklahoma's Murray County and thousands of recreational visitors drawn to the Arbuckle Mountain region's beautiful lake area have relied on Arbuckle Memorial Hospital, in Sulphur, for quality health care since 1959. Over 12,000 patients are served by the critical care hospital annually. One of its biggest challenges in recent years, however, involved its own physical plant. The construction of a new 25-bed, one-story, 50,000-square-foot replacement hospital, designed by Health Facilities Group, was complicated by the need to place the award-winning new facility on the site of the existing one. Health Facilities Group undertook an intricate phasing operation to accommodate the existing hospital and facilitate a smooth transition to its successor. As patients and their families have happily learned, the new steel, masonry, stucco and glass structure and its warm, soothing interior of modern furnishings enable the staff to serve them more effectively than ever. Indeed, more than 5,000 patients are seen each year in the hospital's emergency room, roughly half of all County patients requiring hospitalization are admitted to its nursing unit, and almost half of all County families receive health care from it free of charge through its participation in Sooner Care, a federally funded program.

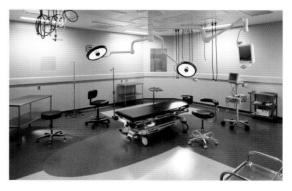

Right, clockwise from top left: Patient room, operating room, atrium exterior, exterior at main entrance, waiting room

Below: Atrium lobby

Photography: Steve Rasmussen

Emergency
Outpatient Services
Medical Records
Patient Rooms

Health Facilities Group, LLC

Labette Health
Parsons, Kansas

A distinguished healthcare institution serving families in Parsons, Kansas and its region for nearly a half century, Labette Health is currently undergoing a comprehensive campus redevelopment program involving 126,000 square feet of renovation and new construction, designed by Health Facilities Group. Upon completion, the project will result in upgraded facilities in the medical office building, wellness center, diabetes education center, all ground floor outpatient services, and pharmacy, and expanded facilities in the surgery department, laboratory, radiology department, dietary, admissions, business office, and central mechanical plant. The project's extensive scope has required a complex phasing operation so that the hospital can remain functional and patients can be safe during the lengthy years of construction. Among the most noticeable changes are the reconfiguration of the entrance and patient flow through the introduction of a central admissions facility that now controls access through the remainder of the departments, and the emergence of light and cheerful modern interiors that enhance the overall healing environment. Assessing the work of Health Facilities Group, William Mahoney, Labette Health's former CEO, declared, "I feel they have done a very good job, and have worked hard to meet our very high expectations. I see them producing big time results."

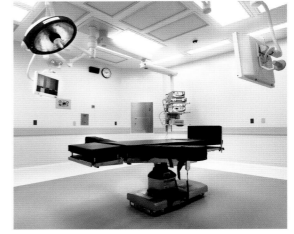

Upper right: Diabetes center entrance

Lower right: Operating room

Below: Reconfigured main entrance

Photography: Labette Health, Health Facilities Group

HGA Architects and Engineers

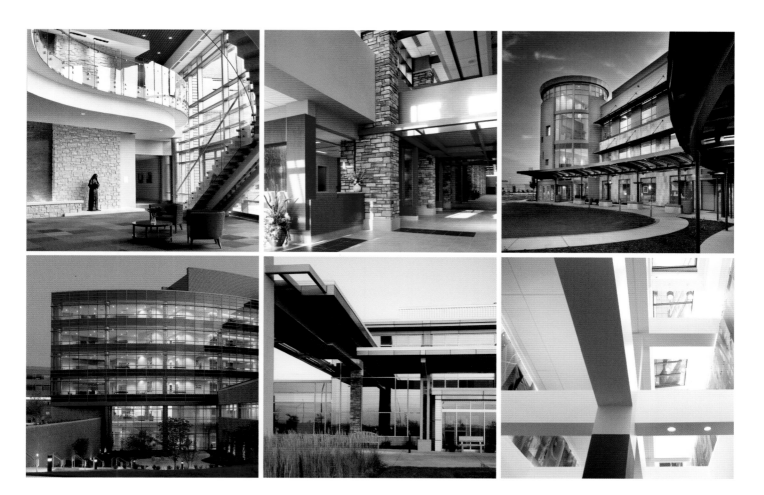

Minneapolis, Minnesota • 612.758.4000

Rochester, Minnesota • 507.281.8600

Milwaukee, Wisconsin • 414.278.8200

Sacramento, California • 916.787.5100

San Francisco, California • 415.814.6910

Los Angeles, California • 310.557.7600

www.hga.com

HGA Architects and Engineers

SSM St. Clare Health Center
Fenton, Missouri

This 430,000-square-foot replacement hospital on a 54-acre site for SSM St. Clare Health Center in Fenton, Missouri, creates a healing, positive environment for patients, visitors and staff. Designed by HGA Architects and Engineers, the facility includes a 174-bed tower, emergency department, surgical suites, outpatient diagnostic, medical office building, ambulatory care center, cancer center and support services . Acknowledging the residential neighborhood, the building nestles into a natural valley below the street level surrounded by green edges. Indoors, spaces incorporate Evidence-Based Design principles. The interior promotes way-finding through a two-story, curved linear spine that links the entry and garden levels while connecting major public areas, including waiting areas, dining, retail services, business center, health-information center, community-shared meeting spaces, and chapel. The Interior further promotes healing with daylight, exterior views to the landscaped campus, fresh contemporary colors, hospitality-inspired furnishings, and private patient

rooms and family areas. Robert G. Porter, president of SSM Health Care, reports that patient volume exceeds projections and patient satisfaction has reached the 87th percentile.

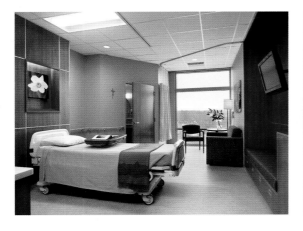

Top: Glass "beacon" welcomes visitors

Above far left, above left: Garden level courtyard, inpatient lobby

Far left, left: Inpatient room, garden level café

Opposite: Main entrance lobby

Photography: Alise O'Brien

114

HGA Architects and Engineers

Sutter Regional Medical Foundation
Medical Office Building 2
Fairfield, California

Needing to vacate a leased space in Fairfield, California, by the end of 2007, Sutter Regional Medical Foundation retained HGA Architects and Engineers to design this three-floor, 70,000-square-foot Medical Office Building #2. HGA finished the project on-time and on-budget thanks to the team's project management skills. The building houses primary care and specialty care suites, laboratories, support services, administrative offices, and clinical facilities for family practice, pediatrics, internal medicine/oncology, cardiology and medical records. The space is easy to navigate and patient-friendly. To help patients with wayfinding, the design features a rotunda that announces the main entrance and offers a generous public concourse on upper floors with outdoor views and access to all departments. The interior finishes include contemporary furnishings, colors derived from nature and energy-efficient direct and indirect lighting to create an attractive, comfortable and practical environment. The result is a win-win for patients and staff of Sutter Regional Medical Foundation, a locally governed and managed affiliate of Sutter Health, a not-for-profit network of physicians and hospitals in northern California.

Right, top to bottom: Public stair, rotunda exterior, entry

Below: Pediatric waiting

Opposite: Upper lobby

Photography: Vance Fox

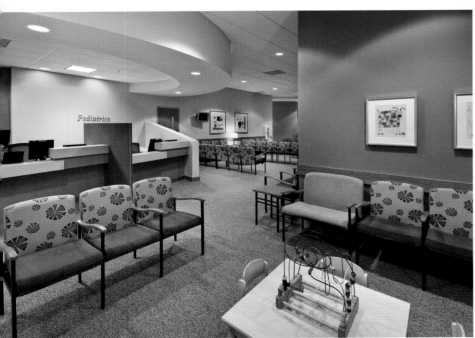

HGA Architects and Engineers

Jefferson County Health Center
Fairfield, Iowa

Communities with Frank Lloyd Wright-designed buildings are rare. So when the Jefferson County Health Center in Fairfield, Iowa, developed its new 120,000-square-foot replacement hospital, it responded to the community's cultural heritage as well as its healthcare needs. Designed by HGA Architects and Engineers, the architecture acknowledges a local Wright-designed home, other historic residences, and an adjacent historic barn site. The Prairie School-inspired contemporary architecture salutes the past with bold forms constructed in cultured stone, brick, composite-metal panel, corrugated metal and glass. A tower and 1½-story public concourse offer visibility from the highway. A garden space, walking trail and picturesque retention pond establishes a generous buffer zone for the historic barn site. The interior architecture extends the Prairie School spirit into spaces that glow with natural light, outdoor views, works of art from local artists, and a sincere respect for patients and the community. The functional floor plan defined by the public concourse and public lobby offers excellent wayfinding to departments that include the emergency department, surgical suite, radiology, medical office building, laboratory, OB clinic, birthing suite, 25-bed inpatient unit and support services.

Above: Public concourse

Left: Exterior showing tower and main entry

Opposite: Entry lobby

Photography: Steve Henke

HGA Architects and Engineers

Cedars-Sinai Medical Center
Samuel Oschin Cancer Center
Los Angeles, California

Below: Skylights and art panels

Bottom left and right: Multiple treatment bays, treatment bay during midday

Right: Art panels

Photography: Tom Bonner

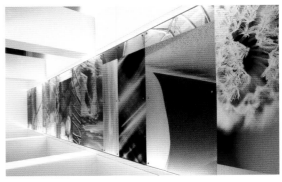

Designed by HGA Architects and Engineers, this 10,000-square-foot expansion to the Infusion Unit at Cedars-Sinai Medical Center Samuel Oschin Cancer Center adds 13 Infusion Bay chairs in a healing environment with strong organizational layout, comforting interior finishes, and improved waiting area. Additionally, acrylic art panels along the vaulted space increase visual interest with multi-colored splashes of natural and supplemental lighting. The Infusion Unit is located in the lower level of the hospital. Daylight streams in from a narrow row of skylights. The design capitalizes on this light source by offering patients pleasing views during their treatment. The softly backlit art panels installed along the upper portions of the east and west walls visually filter daylight deeper into the space. Approximately eight feet tall and four feet wide, each panel depicts colorful images found in nature, selected to represent a sense of life, living, and looking into the future. Synchronized to four-hour cycles that reflect daylight's natural color gradations, supplemental light evolves from rosy red in the morning to white at noon and eventually lavender at sunset. Cedars-Sinai's president Thomas M. Priselac said that the Cancer Center's expansion is "the jewel of the entire facility."

HKS, Inc.

1919 McKinney Avenue • Dallas, TX 75201 • 214.969.5599 • 214.969.3397 (Fax)

www.hksinc.com

HKS, Inc.

University of Arkansas for Medical Sciences
Bed Tower and Parking Garage
Little Rock, Arkansas

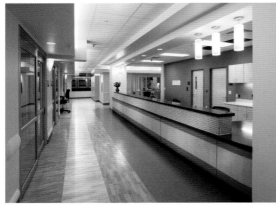

Clockwise from top left:
Patient room, exterior, NICU, waiting area, nurses station

Opposite: Main lobby

Photography: Ed LaCasse

Voted "one of America's best" hospitals by *U.S. News & World Report,* University of Arkansas for Medical Sciences, founded in 1879 in Little Rock, maintains extensive facilities for care, teaching and research. It recently completed a 304-bed, 10-floor, 547,000-square-foot bed tower, designed by HKS, in association with Polk Stanley Wilcox, reflecting its concern that the 50-year-old UAMS Medical Center had become outdated alongside UAMS's centers of excellence. Appropriately, the new, award-winning facility provides a patient-focused environment including state-of-the-art private patient rooms, diagnostic and treatment areas, surgery suites, imaging, emergency department, laboratories, rehabilitation and non-invasive cardiology. Since the tower's positioning atop an underground parking garage required realigning the main drive into the campus, it is also UAMS' new "gateway to healing." Patients and families gratefully notice such features as the sunny, two-story lobby, patient rooms providing custom storage, individually controlled TVs and lighting, and dedicated space and sleeper sofas for visiting family members, extensive family waiting areas throughout offering private coves with views to nature and public seating areas with TVs and café tables, and a roof garden. To quote UAMS chancellor I. Dodd Wilson, M.D., "The opening of the bed tower is the next, much-needed step in the evolution of UAMS."

HKS, Inc.

Salem Hospital
Salem, Oregon

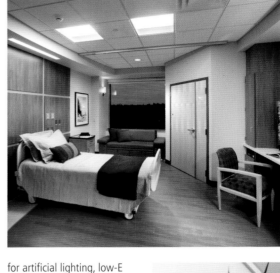

Salem Hospital is a not-for-profit, 454-bed hospital that vividly demonstrates how design is benefiting one of Oregon's largest acute care hospitals. Besides updating and expanding facilities to support advanced treatments and technologies, Salem's new, 120-bed, seven-story, 347,000-square-foot Patient Care Tower, designed by HKS, is enhancing safety, reducing stress, improving effectiveness of care, helping patients and staff to be healthier, and promoting sustainability. The Tower includes an enlarged emergency room, imaging department, surgery and interventional suites, and critical care for patients with heart problems, traumatic injuries and other serious conditions. Because it reflects the findings of evidence-based design research, its environment features good wayfinding, positive distractions, natural views, reduced noise, private, acuity-adaptable rooms, dedicated patient, family and staff spaces, patient- and family-friendly single-patient rooms, family respite spaces, home-like accents, nurturing colors, artwork and staff amenities.

In addition, by embracing the tenants of the Green Guide for Healthcare, it incorporates siting that maximizes views and minimizes mechanical heating and cooling, HVAC equipment that shrinks the building's carbon footprint, daylighting that lowers demand for artificial lighting, low-E glass that cuts energy bills, and xeriscaping and rain and run-off harvesting that save water consumed in landscaping. The hospital demonstrates 21st century health-care in a healing, nurturing and sustainable environment.

Clockwise on both pages, from upper right: Waiting area, main lobby, exterior, landscape, patient room, café

Photography: Blake Marvin/ HKS, Inc.

HKS, Inc.

Seton Medical Center Williamson
Round Rock, Texas

A growing population's need for local, cutting-edge healthcare in Williamson County, Texas has led to the opening of the impressive 125-bed, six-floor, 366,000-square-foot Seton Medical Center Williamson, in Round Rock, designed by HKS. Unique to the not-for-profit Seton Family of Hospitals, a Catholic-affiliated organization founded in 1902 by the Daughters of Charity of St. Vincent de Paul that is the leading healthcare services provider in central Texas, Seton Williamson was planned around the concept of "experience design"—the design and delivery of positive, personal and memorable experiences for patients and their families to improve medical outcomes. Thus, the facility offers surgery, emergency services, radiology and interventional radiology, women's services, NICU and nursery, medical/surgical units, intensive care unit, non-invasive diagnostics, wound care, laboratory, pharmacy, and physical and occupational therapy in a healing environment that supports patients throughout the healing process. Not only does it provide such amenities as rooms that offer low noise, room service, interactive TV, and even a cozy spot for visitors to sleep, it supplements them with such unique elements as a healing garden, waterscape, nature-inspired interiors, specially selected art and a freestanding chapel.

Clockwise on both pages, from upper right: Exterior, patient room, nurses station, main lobby, entry to main lobby

Photography: Blake Marvin/ HKS, inc.

HKS, Inc.

Phoenix Children's Hospital Thomas Campus
Phoenix, Arizona

Demand for pediatric health-care in Phoenix has soared since Phoenix Children's Hospital opened in 1983, and represents a monumental challenge today. Phoenix is America's fifth most populous city, with 970,000 children currently living in metropolitan Phoenix and 1.5 million projected for 2030. Accordingly, the Hospital is implementing a master plan for its main campus at Thomas Road, developed by HKS, that includes a new patient and ambulatory care tower, main entry boulevard, central plant and three parking structures. With family-centered care

in mind, Phoenix Children's has committed to improving the hospital experience for patients and families throughout the phased project. The 334-bed, 11-story, 770,000-square-foot patient and ambulatory care tower, designed by HKS, will be the new campus center. Easy to use, the tower and its welcoming atrium will assemble every resource a patient requires—such as ambulatory care clinics, imaging, surgery, cath lab suite, admitting, all-private patient rooms, pharmacy and cafeteria—replace and expand acute care beds, and reposition Phoenix Children's

for staged replacement and long-term growth. Care has been taken to improve the family journey through lush and whimsical landscaping accentuated with colorful sculpture and soothing water features. The design thoughtfully intertwines indigenous color, playful animal sculptures and desert flowers to visually organize each floor. Strategic day-lighting calms major spaces, punctuates corridors and creates striking vistas within patient rooms. Places of respite capture and integrate the indoors and outdoors.

Top: Exterior
Above: Clinic waiting area
Left: Atrium
Illustration: Courtesy of HKS, Inc.
Photography: Blake Marvin/ HKS, Inc.

HMC Architects

633 West 5th Street, Third Floor • Los Angeles, California 90071 • 213.542.8300 • 213.542.8301 (Fax)

www.hmcarchitects.com

HMC Architects

Kaiser Permanente Downey Medical Center
Downey, California

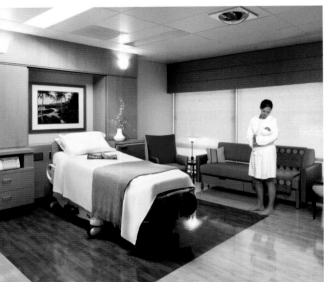

Above: Exterior
Far left: Patient room
Left: Café
Lower left: Waiting room
Opposite: Atrium
Photography: David Lena

Taking advantage of its proximity to an existing primary care facility, the new, 352-bed, six-story, 658,000-square-foot Kaiser Permanente Downey Medical Center, designed by HMC Architects, introduces an impressive, comprehensive care facility. The hospital works with Kaiser Permanente's outpatient garden and orchard medical office buildings to welcome southeast Los Angeles County residents into an environment that is both patient-friendly and effective.

Its appeal is enhanced by floor plans that promote wayfinding and spaces that support patients and families. For example, a daylighted central concourse guides patients on a broad path that spans from the existing clinics, new plaza, parking structure and gardens to the new medical center's entry and emergency department drop-off, as well as pharmacies, imaging, clinical lab, member services, elevators, gift shop, and cafeteria. Furthermore, more than 95 percent of beds occupy spacious private

rooms featuring pull-out beds for overnight visitors, thereby reducing patient stress and improving medical outcomes. Sustainability features include generous windows, carpeting made from recycled materials, an air system using 100 percent fresh air, and paints free of toxic materials. In short, the hospital will serve the Los Angeles community with distinction for years to come.

HMC Architects

The First People's Hospital, Shunde District
Guangzhou Province
People's Republic of China

Left: Aerial view of campus

Below: Patient tower

Bottom: Main entrance

Opposite: Central atrium/spine

Illustrations: Courtesy of Guangzhou Frontop Digital Technology Co. LTD

The 2,000-bed, 2.4-million-square-foot complex and 400,000-square-foot parking structure now being developed as The First People's Hospital, designed by HMC Architects in association with the Shunde Architectural Design Institute of China, integrates the West's latest design and planning ideas with the East's best practices. Regional perspectives in medical planning and building design show up everywhere, including public spaces, patient rooms, perioperative platform, patient flow and more. The campus' future development similarly anticipates a local approach to funding, code compliance, departmental growth, turnkey implementation, and technology usage. In addition, as one of China's first sustainable hospitals, the project incorporates such features as solar screening devices, green roofs, geothermal heat pump exchange, bioswales, photovoltaic systems, and local building materials and interior finishes. Despite its complexity, the award-winning design represents an attractive and patient-friendly environment. Its open campus layout features a linear arrangement of buildings connected by a central atrium/spine runs through the entire medical campus.

In optimizing site efficiency and minimizing infection control risks, the independent but interconnected blocks extend a sincere welcome to the people of Shunde.

HMC Architects

Kaiser Permanente West Los Angeles Medical Center
West Wing Tower Addition
Los Angeles, California

Seamless as the connection appears between the existing tower and its new, 106-bed, five-story, 203,000-square-foot addition, designed by HMC Architects, the construction tells a more challenging story. A 60-foot-long, connecting corridor spans above existing underground utilities to join the old and new structures, and a thorough consolidation and reconfiguration of inpatient, outpatient-, and acute-care functions, prompted by the expansion, enhance efficiency and patient care. The project is one of the first Kaiser hospitals to adopt the Templates 2000 program, which is the country's largest not-for-profit health plan developed to capture and codify best practices for all departmental rooms, equipment, planning, and functional programs. Employing the basic Templates 2000 "kit of parts" to extend and upgrade the existing bed tower, HMC Architects has created a patient-focused facility with attractive, modern spaces characterized by curved elements, soft colors, hospitality-inspired furnishings, and sophisticated direct and indirect lighting. Effective wayfinding helps

Above: Exterior

Below: Main entrance lobby

Opposite: Canopy at main entrance

Photography: David Lena

patients and their families navigate the facility, starting with the curbside canopy at the new patient drop-off and continuing through the new main lobby and other public spaces, with circulation paths that lead to departmental reception areas, waiting rooms, and all-private patient rooms. Sensitivity to the needs of patients and their families makes the facility particularly inviting and supportive, providing such patient room details as generous space for family members, sofa beds for overnight stays, storage space for personal belongings, residential-style wood cabinetry, and paneling surrounding headwalls. The non-clinical ambiance alleviates the inevitable stress of patients and visitors surrounded by medical equipment. Accompanied by a new site circulation plan, new patient drop-off, new pedestrian plaza, and new meditation garden, this addition reassuringly demonstrates that bigger can still be better in 21st-century healthcare.

Below left and right: Patient room, departmental reception and waiting area

Bottom left and right: Major corridor, post-op area

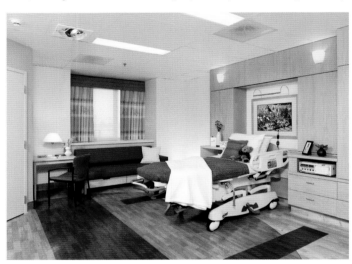

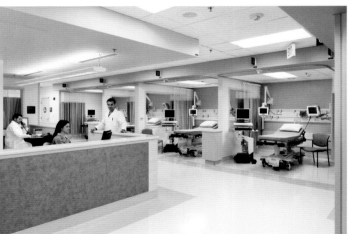

HOK

620 Avenue of the Americas, 6th Floor • New York, NY 10011 • 212.981.7316 • 212.633.1163 (Fax)

www.hok.com

HOK

Methodist Stone Oak Hospital
San Antonio, Texas

Advances in hospital design that anticipate rapidly evolving ways to diagnose and treat patients are creatively employed in the "Hospital of the Future," the exciting new, 132-bed, five-floor, 400,000-square-foot Methodist Stone Oak Hospital, occupying a 50-acre site in San Antonio, Texas, designed by HOK for Methodist Healthcare System of San Antonio and Hospital Corporation of America. Perhaps its most significant concept is the organization of outpatient care so patients arrive for procedures at Centers of Excellence organized along an Outpatient Services Mall, a concourse where key campus programs are readily identified through architecture and signage. This arrangement permits more care to be delivered in settings appropriate to acuity level, easier public access, efficient grouping of services, improved pre- and post-procedure care, and cost-effective and minimally disruptive expansion. Simultaneously, the design introduces state-of-the-art, family-focused inpatient spaces that promote high-end, hospitality-style experiences despite conservative budgets, including stylish yet comfortable patient rooms that meet all infection control objectives, facilitate caregivers and accommodate families. According to Stone Oak's CNO and COO, Jeannette Skinner, RN, "Patients and potential practitioners report that the design for the concourse and exterior is a deciding factor in choosing where to receive care or practice."

Above: Waiting area
Below: Mall
Right: Exterior
Opposite top, left to right: Café, patient room, chapel
Photography: Paul Rivera/archphoto

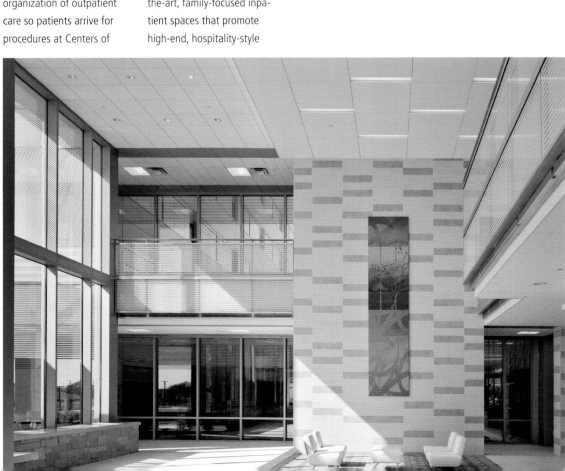

HOK

Community Hospital of the Monterey Peninsula
The Pavilions Project
Monterey, California

Left, clockwise from upper left: Reception desk, patient room with TV wall, forest view from patient room, main lobby seen from exterior

Below left: Main lobby

Opposite: Exterior with healing garden

Photography: Lawrence Anderson

Few hospital settings could rival the 22-acre forest of Monterey pines surrounding Community Hospital of the Monterey Peninsula, in Monterey, California, which borders scenic Holman Highway, the Pacific Ocean and legendary Pebble Beach golf course. It's a distinction the 76-year-old institution treasures. Thus, the recently completed, four-floor (plus three-level underground parking), 290,000-square-foot Pavilions Project, an expansion and renovation comprising the 120-bed, 100,000-square-foot Forest Pavilion, 100,000-square-foot South Pavilion, centralizing critical care departments, and 90,000 square feet of modernized space, was designed by HOK to respect the landscape and 100-bed, 210,000-square-foot 1962 building designed by Edward Durell Stone. HOK worked with the community to address site concerns, establishing visual setbacks from public roads, maintaining view corridors, and relocating specimen trees only when necessary. The new, award-winning design maintains the original scale, sweeping rooflines and Neoclassic modernism of Stone's architecture while updating the all-white interiors with state-of-the-art facilities, cherry wood accents, and patient-centered accommodations such as spacious patient rooms with full-height wardrobes, daybeds for families and views of the forest or new healing garden. Complimenting HOK's skill in blending its additions with Stone's building while resolving sensitive site issues, hospital president Dr. Steven Packer proclaimed, "HOK accomplished this task admirably."

HOK

Royal National Orthopedic Hospital NHS Trust
Central London Outpatient Assessment Centre
London, United Kingdom

A renowned national center of excellence for the United Kingdom's National Health Service, the Royal National Orthopaedic Hospital NHS Trust provides a comprehensive range of neuro-musculo-skeletal health care, ranging from the most acute spinal injury or complex bone tumor to orthopedic medicine and specialist rehabilitation, for chronic back pain sufferers. The hospital's sparkling new three-level, 20,000-square-foot Central London Outpatient Assessment Centre, designed by HOK, houses clinics, imaging, orthotics, occupational therapy, physiotherapy, pre-operative assessment and plaster services. Its state-of-the-art treatment facilities work in tandem with an exceptional healing environment, establishing a welcoming and inspirational space, helping patients minimize waiting time and find their destination, providing flexibility, and smoothly integrating with a residential mixed-use development. From the glass curtain wall that maintains contact with the streetscape to the spatial clarity that features circulation areas that are places in their own right, original works of art that celebrate the human skeletal structure, and bright and cheerful modern furnishings and floor-wide color themes that orient patients and put them at ease, the Centre gives modern medicine a compassionate face. As CEO Rob Hurd has declared, "The Centre is a fantastic facility for patients and represents the clinical excellence undertaken at the RNOH."

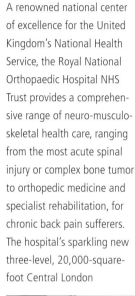

Top left, right: Receptionist, wall mural

Far left: Exterior

Left: Waiting room

Opposite top: Main entrance

Photography: Paul Grundy

HOK

Alberta Health Services
Peter Lougheed Centre
Calgary, Alberta, Canada

Peter Lougheed Centre, a component of Alberta Health Services, provides vital care to Calgary's rapidly growing, ethnically diverse northeast community. Accordingly, the design and management team currently directing its six-story, 398,265-square-foot east wing expansion and 107,000-square-foot renovation, designed by HOK in collaboration with Marshall Tittemore Architects, regularly engages residents in dialogue, discussing its intentions in sustainable design, operating principles, cleaning systems and recycling methods. The project will provide new or improved facilities, including diagnostics imaging core, high-technology operating rooms, intensive care unit, cardiac care unit, hemodialysis unit, mental health clinics, mental health short stay, transplant clinic, transplant and renal inpatient unit, clinical laboratory services, and emergency department, to handle population growth and greater outpatient care. Registered as a LEED program, it will offer such sustainable features as operable windows, patient room daylighting, non-VOC-bearing building materials, and energy-efficient mechanical systems. To effectively maintain infection control, it will employ rubber flooring and other easily cleaned surfaces, mold-resistant drywall, patient room hand-washing sinks, in-room bedpan cleaners and safety zones that can easily isolate component areas. Equally important, Peter Lougheed Centre will deliver quality services in a patient-focused environment that demonstrates Canada's largest health care provider can satisfy its varied constituents.

Far left: Family lounge
Left: Intensive care unit
Below left: Exterior of east wing extension
Photography: Richard Johnson

Horty Elving

505 East Grant Street • Minneapolis, MN 55404 • 612.332.4422 • 612.344.1282 (Fax)

www.hortyelving.com

Horty Elving

St. Anthony Regional Hospital
Surgery Center
Carroll, Iowa

Right: Exterior

Below: Corridor

Below right: Outpatient recovery room

Opposite: Atrium

Photography: Dale Photographics

Founded in 1905 by Reverend Joseph Kuemper with the assistance of the Franciscan Sisters of Perpetual Adoration, St. Anthony Regional Hospital & Nursing Home, in Carroll, Iowa, is a 99-bed facility and 79-bed nursing home serving west central Iowa with physicians in many specialties, state-of-the-art equipment and up-to-date treatment procedures. Its new, four-story, 120,000-square-foot inpatient/outpatient/Surgical Unit, designed by Horty Elving, replaces 35-year-old facilities with a surgery/endoscopic center where four operating rooms, two shelled future surgery spaces, two endoscopy suites, and 20 private ambulatory recovery rooms handle both inpatients and outpatients while keeping them separated. To do this, the new structure matches the existing hospital's elevations, connecting on the first floor via an underground tunnel, and via skybridges—the surgery center where all surgical services are located—to the main medical/surgical inpatient floor and the fourth floor to the future orthopedic surgery floor. This scheme allows surgeons, staff and patients of surgery and the adjoining surgery clinics to park on the first and second floors of the new structure and reach the surgery center directly via elevator. (The underground passage links the new structure to the hospital's emergency/radiology services, establishing

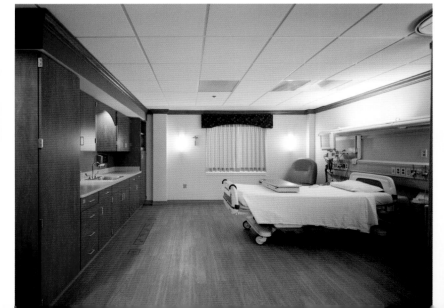

direct private transport from emergency to the third floor, and materials management.) Interiors reflect simultaneous concern for effective operations and patient wellbeing. Surgery rooms, for example, encompass about 800 square feet each and are identical in design and equipment orientation, with operating rooms offering robotics and other advanced technologies. In addition, outpatient

recovery rooms are all private rooms, many combining comfort with spectacular views of the surrounding countryside. Daylight harvesting illuminates many staff, recovery and public spaces with natural light, a surgery information system keeps families informed of patients' status during the surgery process. Comfortable, understated furnishings and sophisticated lighting

enhance the experience of patients, family members and friends, highlighted by warm wood finishes in patient areas. Thanks to the new facility, patients in the Carroll area can receive state-of-the-art surgical services without journeying two hours to a major metropolitan area.

Below: Examination room
Right: Surgery waiting room
Opposite top left and right: Nurses station, atrium

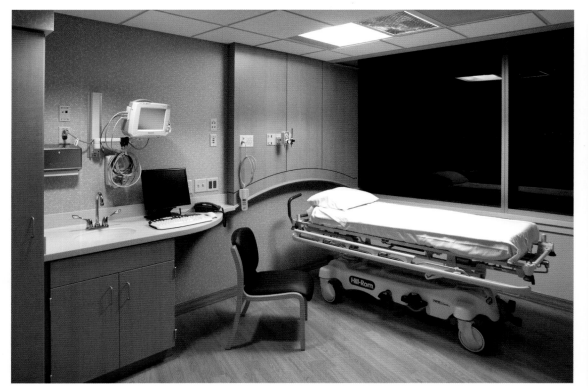

Horty Elving

Warroad Senior Living Center
Warroad, Minnesota

If life is a journey, the new Warroad Senior Living Center, in Warroad, Minnesota, offers a one-story, 97,663-square-foot residential facility, designed by Horty Elving, full of creative and rewarding ways to re-imagine the journey. The Center incorporates 49 beds of skilled nursing, 22 units of assisted living, 10 units of memory care assisted living and 22 units of independent living in an integrated campus that supports the elderly at their specific level of need. While independent living residents are likely to participate in community life outside the Center, skilled nursing residents are likely to regard the Center as both home and community. The facility is "de-institutionalized" to feel like home to all residents. Thus, each resident has a private room within a household that exists within a neighborhood, with neighborhoods collectively forming the community. What unites everyone is the lodge center, where a den, fitness center, movie theater, barber/beauty shop, therapy and dining rooms host shared and community activities. Equally universal in appeal is the Center's Northern Minnesota Lodge theme, establishing a world of architecture and landscape where ease of use, support, durability and maintainability coexist with warmth, comfort, quality and tradition, and porches, gardens, ponds and courtyards incorporate the outdoors into everyday experience.

Top: Exterior at main public entrance

Left: Lodge center

Above, clockwise from upper left: Great room with fireplace, café, town center patio, enclosed porch

Photography: Markert Photo

Horty Elving

Brown County Community Treatment Center
Green Bay, Wisconsin

While its Prairie-style architecture of stone, wood and glass projects an appropriately warm and reassuring image, the new Brown County Community Treatment Center, in Green Bay, Wisconsin, is actually a complex healthcare facility combining a psychiatric hospital, long-term care facility and outpatient mental health clinic. Designed by Horty Elving, the one-story, 103,700-square-foot facility includes 35 beds for the psychiatric hospital and 63 beds for long-term care as well as the mental health clinic. The long-term care facility represents a cultural change in skilled nursing to a "neighborhood concept," replacing long, double-loaded corridors with "neighborhoods" where "households" have their own living rooms, dining rooms, bathing areas and private rooms for each of 10 residents per household. To streamline and consolidate services, the psychiatric hospital also houses the County's detox unit, including a judge's chambers and small court that permit civil commitment and criminal hearings for patients without needing to transport them; the hospital's connection to the outpatient mental health clinic benefits inpatients by enabling them to see the same mental health professional as outpatients. The commitment of client and designer to the Center once again demonstrates that outstanding healthcare facilities are feasible despite formidable complexity and constraint.

Jain Malkin Inc.

5070 Santa Fe Street • San Diego, CA 92109 • 858.454.3377 • 858.272.6199 (Fax)

www.jainmalkin.com

Jain Malkin Inc.

Eisenhower Medical Center
Greg and Stacey Renker Pavilion
Rancho Mirage, California

Right: Suite family area
Far right: Library
Below: Reception
Photography: Steve McClelland

Close by southern California's legendary Palm Springs, Eisenhower Medical Center, in Rancho Mirage, is the recipient of substantial philanthropic gifts from prominent families who maintain winter homes in the region, resulting in new facilities, advanced diagnostic imaging equipment and robotic surgical devices. Four years ago, Eisenhower's CEO decided to honor the benefactors by creating a nursing unit of 24 patient and guest suites to provide the best possible experience when they or their families need inpatient services.

The result is the one-floor, 35,548-square-foot Greg and Stacey Renker Pavilion, developed by a team comprising Moon Mayoras Architects, architect, Jain Malkin Inc., interior architecture, lighting design, art consulting and overall design lead, Syska & Hennessy, MEP engineering, Turner Construction Company, construction, and Harmon Nelson, environmental graphics. The unique setting of the Renker Pavilion, offering a level of design and amenities appropriate to upscale boutique hotels, transforms the hospital experience by employing hospitality design concepts to enhance the healing process. For example, patient and guest amenities—including library, business center, consultation rooms, family room/game area and private family dining—are integrated so families and friends can actively participate in

155

Jain Malkin Inc.

patient care. In addition, private rooms for family and guest use are joined by an architecturally distinctive connector, family members and other visitors have their own bathroom, a gourmet kitchen and personal chef are available upon request, and high-profile design, usually limited to the lobby in healthcare facilities, extends to patient suites as well.

Each patient suite comes with fine furnishings, art, and such luxury hotel amenities as custom-designed bed linens, Italian marble bathroom with spa rain shower, entertainment center with flat screen television, DVD player, headphones and surround sound, desk with Internet link, kitchenette with mini-bar refrigerator, microwave and safe, custom sleeper

sofa and lounge chairs, contemporary lighting, ample closets and luggage racks. Not surprisingly, the array of desirable features in the Renker Pavilion powerfully demonstrates the built environment's potential impact on a patient's healing experience and medical outcome. Research in the neurosciences, specifically psychoneuroimmunology (concerning

the impact of emotions on the immune system), indicates that a comfortable, low-stress healthcare environment can lead to less post-operative bleeding, less blood loss during surgery, reduced perception of pain, and earlier discharge. "Our Press Ganey scores are 99 percentile," notes Linda Sakai, director of the Renker Pavilion. "Patients describe

their rooms as 'amazing,' 'not at all like a hospital,' 'very private and quiet,' and 'promotes healing.'"

Top: Patient room
Above: Corridor
Left: Shower area
Far left: Nurse station

Jain Malkin Inc.

Cisco LifeConnections Health Center
San Jose, California

Cisco Systems, the global leader in networking equipment, has demonstrated its leadership anew by developing an outstanding healthcare program for employees. On the campus of Cisco's headquarters in San Jose, California, the Cisco LifeConnections Health Center, a new, two-story, 24,000-square-foot freestanding facility, designed by a project team comprising Jain Malkin Inc., clinic planner, interior architect and lighting designer, IA Interior Architects, executive architect, CBRE, project manager, Brightworks, LEED design consultant, and Devcon Construction, general contractor, improves the wellbeing of employees and their families through health care, child care and fitness. The LEED Gold-certified facility promotes wellness by immersing patients in a comfortable, spa-like healthcare clinic embedded with a high level of technology. The clinic offers primary care along with acupuncture, travel medicine, mental health, nutrition counseling, chiropractic, physical therapy, pharmacy, laboratory and radiology in an orthogonal network of perimeter and interior spaces anchored by four 12-foot diameter rotundas or "inspirational nodes" with glazed light wells and major corridors that widen as they near the

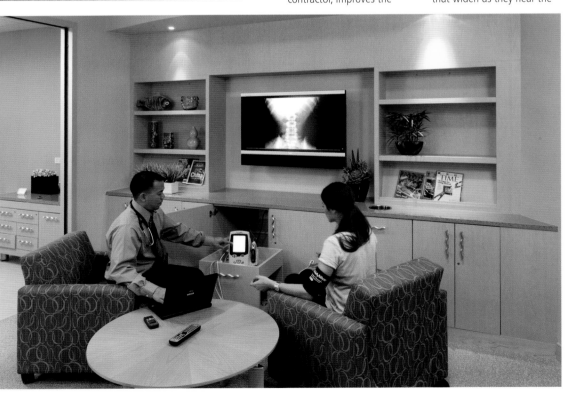

Below: Lobby

Opposite: Corridor

Opposite bottom: Patient
care suite

Photography: Steve McClelland

Jain Malkin Inc.

exterior to admit more daylight. Despite the density of the space, openness prevails, promoted by the second-story location, overlooking treetops, and mirrors at the top of corridor walls that touch the wood grid ceiling, making the ceiling appear to continue beyond the walls. Yet the clinic's operations are as impressive as its spaces because the patient experience has been painstakingly mapped, both spatially and digitally. For example, patients check-in electronically and proceed to the next available care suite, where their vital signs are captured and automatically uploaded to the electronic health record, to be shared via the wall monitor with care providers whose badges activate the screen system. According to Pamela Hymel, the Center's medical director, this extraordinary facility will pay for itself through increased productivity and reduced benefit costs in just a few years.

Clockwise, from top left: Acrylic sculpture wall in lobby, informal seating in staff corridor, examination room, inspirational node

Mitchell Associates

Mitchell Associates

Harford Memorial Hospital
Havre de Grace, Maryland

Serving the people of historic Havre de Grace, Maryland since 1910, Harford Memorial Hospital recently found itself needing to update the interiors of its circa-1950 building. Aware that studies in evidence-based design are affirming the role that healing environments play in improving medical outcomes, but lacking money for extensive renovations, the hospital asked Mitchell Associates to develop creative and cost effective design solutions. To overcome the project's constraints, the design employs finishes that are timeless, appealing and durable; millwork that combines aesthetics, flexibility and low maintenance; and lighting that uses the existing grid to introduce new direct and indirect fixtures, including overbed lights and decorative sconces. The results have been very gratifying. Patient rooms for example, provide brighter, more colorful and friendlier settings for patients, families and staff. Nurses stations have exchanged chipped and peeling millwork for more flexible modular furniture workstations. Patient elevator lobbies are enlivened by full-height photo murals of recognizable local scenes in Harford County that introduce comforting, familiar images and aid wayfinding. Although the cafeteria still remains in a windowless basement space, the installation of photo murals, vinyl flooring mimicking wood planks, and sophisticated lighting has transformed it into an underground spring garden.

Clockwise from bottom right:
Entry lobby (before and after), cafeteria (before and after), elevator lobby, photo mural

Photography: Mitchell Associates

Mitchell Associates

Erickson Living at Ann's Choice
Community Building
Warminster, Pennsylvania

Erickson Living is a successful developer and operator of retirement communities housing over 22,000 people on 19 campuses in Colorado, Illinois, Kansas, Maryland, Massachusetts, Michigan, New Jersey, Pennsylvania, Texas, and Virginia. Based in Baltimore County, Maryland since 1983, Erickson attracts people to its "worry-free lifestyle" that includes on-site amenities. These include restaurants, stores, fitness centers with full-time trainers, and medical centers staffed by board-certified primary care physicians specializing in geriatrics, along with such everyday services as transportation, grounds maintenance, and housekeeping. At Ann's Choice, a new Erickson development in Warminster, Pennsylvania, Mitchell Associates has designed the two-floor, 49,000-square-foot interior of the community building to create a welcoming, comfortable and distinctly residential-style environment. The community building encloses a fireplace lounge, dining room, game room/bar, pharmacy and administrative offices in an environment that promotes wayfinding, social activity and relaxation through window-lined corridors, spatial settings for both intimate and group gatherings, and a small-scaled, informal and carefully detailed transitional interior design. Stressing vernacular style, utility and durability, the furnishings combine wood and upholstered furniture, wood millwork, carpet, wood plank-style vinyl flooring, vinyl wallcovering, solid surfacing and hospitality-inspired lighting. Residents like the dining room so much they say it resembles a fine restaurant.

Clockwise, both pages, from top left: Dining room entrance, dining room detail, fireplace lounge, bedroom, view through interior window, corridor

Photography: Madeline Fucile, Mitchell Associates

Mitchell Associates

Alfred I. duPont Hospital for Children
Family Resource Center and Child Life Facility
Wilmington, Delaware

Seriously ill children from the nation and the world have found their way to the Alfred I. duPont Hospital for Children, in Wilmington, Delaware, since its founding in 1940. The hospital is a division of Nemours, one of the nation's largest subspecialty group practices devoted to pediatric patient care, teaching, and research. Thanks to two new facilities nestled in the heart of the 180-bed institution, the Family Resource Center and Child Life Facility, both designed by Mitchell Associates, families now have unique, on-site accommodations that let them remain together during their child's stay. While the 7,000-square-foot Family Resource Center functions as a home-away-from-home space by providing a lounge, kitchen, laundry, library, educational lecture room, "hands-on" training room, sleep rooms and showers, the adjoining, 2,000-square-foot Child Life space acts as the hospital's playroom with amenities that include an activity kitchen, arts and crafts, movies and games, toddler zone, teen center and Child Life administrative offices. Forms, materials, colors and lighting are all orchestrated to create a satisfying experience for children and adults alike. In the sleep rooms, for example, diffused lighting, subtly patterned carpet and soft-toned walls in woodland hues give fatigued parents a safe haven just when they need it most.

Above: Corridor
Top right: Entertainment center
Right: Seating area
Photography: Mitchell Associates

Mitchell Associates

Nouveau Medispa
Newark, Delaware

Owned and operated by physicians practicing at Christiana Hospital, in Newark, Delaware, the Advanced Plastic Surgery Center recently expanded beyond reconstructive surgery to serve a cosmetic and health spa clientele. Its new, one-floor, 8,000-square-foot Nouveau Medispa, designed by Mitchell Associates, lets the physicians retain their existing business as a separate entity, share staff and administrative facilities, and work in either practice from one central pivot point. To entice existing clients, Nouveau Medispa reveals itself discreetly to them at selected points. Its airy, comfortable and stylish space, housing a reception area, examination rooms, day spa rooms, doctors' offices, nurses administration, laundry and lunchroom, offers luxurious accommodations, amenities that heighten the senses, and a holistic healing experience. For example, adjoining the hotel-style reception area is a juice bar, a cozy niche showcasing skincare products, and a warm, gold-toned conference room, doubling as a dining room when necessary. An eight-foot-tall, luminous, custom-designed partition of curved acrylic and glass separates the scheduling waiting area from the receptionist's desk, crafted of the same maple and marble as the custom-designed reception desk. From the flow of space and light to the colors, materials and furnishings, everything declares that patients are pampered guests here.

Top left and right: Day spa rooms

Right: Reception area with lunchroom at left and director's office in rear

Photography: Pearce

Mitchell Associates

Christiana Project
Helen F. Graham Cancer Center, Cyberknife Facility
Newark, Delaware

Christiana Care's Helen F. Graham Cancer Center, on the Newark, Delaware campus of 913-bed Christiana Hospital, is a state-of-the-art facility that treats a majority of Delaware's cancer patients. A National Cancer Institute-designated Community Cancer Center, it serves as a model for other healthcare systems, enrolling more cancer patients in clinical trials than in most other programs in the nation. To conduct its work, it features advanced medical technology, including the Cyberknife Robotic Radiosurgery System and the Da Vinci Robotic

Surgery System, along with a laboratory where cancer researchers and oncologists collaborate in developing new treatments, and comprehensive services and amenities for cancer diagnosis and treatment. The accommodations are as patient-friendly as they are effective, including the 3,000-square-foot Cyberknife facility, designed by Mitchell Associates. Patients enter a maze-like entrance and encounter hand-blown pendant lighting fixtures, wood floors with decorative inlays, and soft colors, all evoking the ambience of an upscale hotel, en

route to the Cyberknife unit. Once a patient is inside the unit, he or she is surrounded by a 360-degree view of murals of the local countryside, complete with a sky image overhead. Patients are responding positively to the environment, one even comparing her visit to a day at the spa.

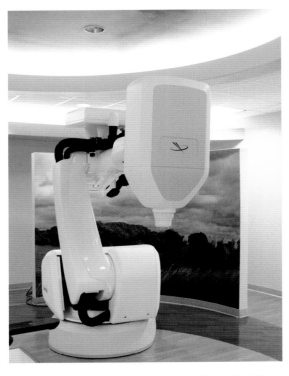

Above and left: Cyberknife equipment and facility
Photography: Christiana Care

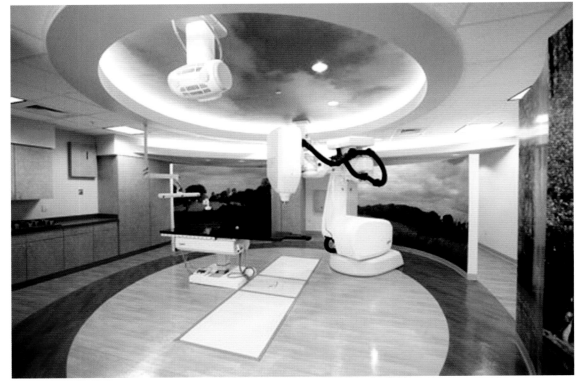

NBBJ

NBBJ

Swedish Orthopedic Institute
Seattle, Washington

Because healthcare relies on trust and openness between patients and care providers, Seattle's esteemed Swedish Medical Center asked NBBJ to design its Orthopedic Institute as an open, stress-free environment to improve recovery time and ease the transition from hospital to home. The award-winning, seven-story, 372,000-square-foot facility lets patients experience state-of-the-art treatment and technology in a transparent atmosphere of daylight, visual connections and improved wayfinding. Comprising 10 operating rooms, 28-bed prep/recovery area, inpatient nursing units, outpatient care, education and training facilities, preadmissions testing center, pharmacy, café, sterile processing area and parking garage, the Institute reveals the healing process to patients and community in various ways. Since inpatients are transferred up to six times during typical orthopedic procedures, often feeling disoriented, the new space creates an intuitive, easy-to-navigate experience so they can progress seamlessly, comforted by a consistency of form and materials and continuous outdoor connection—with over half the glass, metal, stone and wood-clad building lit by direct daylight. For the community, the design defines a new front door to the south side of the Swedish campus and builds connections through improved campus edges, pedestrian paths, landscaped gardens and a building geometry respecting the neighborhood's character and scale.

Below left: Naturally-lit pre-op area
Bottom left: Patient room
Below: Main lobby
Opposite: Two-story glass entry pavillion
Photography: Benjamin Benschneider

NBBJ

Providence Park Hospital
Novi, Michigan

Providence Park Hospital is described by its owner system, St. John Health System of southeast Michigan, as "The Hospital of the Future. Today." While this resounds with parental pride, the new 220-bed, six-story, 496,000-square-foot is nonetheless exceptionally patient-focused. Designed by NBBJ to incorporate best practices in both healthcare and hospitality, Providence Park engages patients and families coming to the nation's largest variable-acuity hospital with a soothing healing environment offering differentiated inpatient and outpatient experiences. Highlights include 200 private patient rooms that accommodate families; dedicated buildings for outpatient services; onstage/offstage design (from the Disney Institute) separating patient, caregiver and materials movement from public areas; flexible interventional/ surgical center with universally-sized surgery suites; Women's and Infant Health Center with 27 LDRP rooms; 49 bed-Emergency Center with dedicated imaging services; and a progressive healthy food/nutrition program. Providence Park is also a key addition to a new destination site shared with an Orthopedic Center and Ambulatory Surgical Center, medical office building and Neurosciences Institute, 1.6-mile outdoor fitness path, hotel, and Town Center incorporating residential and retail units. In evaluating the project, Providence Park's president Rob Cassalou concludes, "The NBBJ team invested time and resources into truly capturing the goals we intended for the campus."

Abovr, clockwise from upper left: Connection corridor, exterior, atrium lobby, reception

Photography: © Tom Arban

NBBJ

Southcentral Foundation, Primary Care Clinic III
Anchorage, Alaska

Southcentral Foundation's new, three-story, 75,000-square-foot facility, Primary Care Clinic III, designed by NBBJ, is as outstanding as the organization it serves. Incorporated in 1982 as an Alaska Native owned healthcare organization, Southcentral Foundation serves some 46,800 Alaska Native and American Indian people in greater Anchorage. The PCC III freestanding addition builds upon concepts tested in PCC II to create a gathering place as well as a point of entry, and

reinforces Southcentral's ability to have Integrated Care Teams of professionals treat patients rather than send them to find specialized care. To do this, the Native Alaskan culture-inspired interiors provide a sensitive, non-clinical transition from public space to semi-public, semi-private and private space. Care Teams work in large, open spaces on the building's outer edge, and conduct private examinations in flexible facilities called Talking Rooms that avoid examination tables while

encouraging conversations among patient, family members and caregivers. Similarly, lobbies on each floor accommodate families; education and resource areas with computer stations give patients access to resource data; and staff workstations let Care Team members collaborate in promoting patients' wellness. Joe Federici, Southcentral's vice president, behavioral services division, lauds the design's ability "to create environments that foster pride and self-esteem."

Right: Reception
Far right: Atrium and stair
Below: Exterior entry
Below right: Entry canopy
Photography: Benjamin Benschneider

NBBJ

Cleveland Clinic
Arnold & Sydell Miller Family Pavilion
and Glickman Tower
Cleveland, Ohio

Since prominence in cardiovascular disease first drew worldwide attention to the Cleveland Clinic, a renowned nonprofit multi-specialty academic medical center founded in 1921 in Cleveland that integrates clinical and hospital care with research and education, it is fitting that the new homes of the Miller Family Heart and Vascular Institute and Glickman Urological Institute provide a new front door on Euclid Avenue to the Clinic's 140-acre campus. The 10-story, 987,000-square-foot Miller Pavilion and 12-story, 300,000-square-foot Glickman Tower are designed by NBBJ as integral components of the campus. They also function as a gateway between the existing Crile Building mall and 93rd Street boulevard, with the Miller Pavilion emulating the curve of the large quarter-circle that opens to the street

and embracing the spacious entrance plaza and patient drop-off area to be shared with the Clinic's Children's Hospital and Main Hospital. Their facilities are extensive, including a main lobby, patient check-in lounge, 278 private patient rooms, 16 operating rooms, 12 catheterization laboratories, 13 nuclear medicine rooms, 110 intensive care beds, 208 examination rooms, 95 procedure rooms, 230 physicians' offices, conference center, resource center, retail and more. Besides offering the means for effective, state-of-the-art operations, the award-winning design focuses on establishing strong patient and family

Right, in descending order: Miller Pavilion main lobby, enclosed circulation path, chapel

Opposite: Exterior at entrance plaza

Photography: Paul Warchol, Benjamin Benschneider, Tom Arban

174

orientation, reaffirming the Clinic's "Healing Hospitality" brand, and creating a new brand/image for the Clinic. To orient patients and families, the design introduces such visual landmarks as atriums and a winter garden and minimizes the visual clutter that characterizes typical hospitals through elegant, understated interiors. The Miller Pavilion extends the Clinic's "Healing Hospitality" by providing the patient with a superior experience from point of arrival to patient room and beyond, combining healthcare and hospitality design concepts to produce an attractive, high-quality

and friendly ambiance. A new brand/image is achieved for the Clinic by having the Miller Pavilion reach into the community by curving to form the new entrance plaza and tying it to a circulation concept developed around an existing winter garden, composing what could become an iconic view of the Clinic.

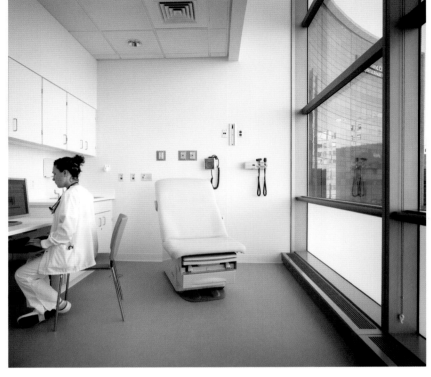

Right: Examination room
Below: Patient room
Photography: Benjamin Benschneider

PageSoutherlandPage

Austin • Dallas • Denver • Houston • Washington, DC

www.pspaec.com

PageSoutherlandPage

Baylor Regional Medical Center at Plano
Plano, Texas

Since opening in 2004, 160-bed Baylor Regional Medical Center at Plano, in Plano, Texas, continually develops new services and building space on its 29-acre site to meet healthcare needs in North Texas, with master planning, programming, design and engineering by PageSoutherlandPage. Baylor Plano currently comprises a first phase, including a 354,400-square-foot hospital, 195,000-square-foot medical office building, 1,080-vehicle parking garage, central energy plant and related surface parking and site improvements, and a second phase, including a 149,510-square-foot medical office building and 1,075-vehicle parking garage. Part of 107-year-old Baylor University Medical Center, the complex is distinguished by its efficient configuration, maximizing limited acreage and optimizing access and adjacencies, as well as its patient-focused environment, where patients are treated as guests in a hotel-like experience. Among its many popular features are excellent wayfinding, the terraced healing garden bordering the glass-enclosed dining facility, spacious, attractive and family-friendly private patient rooms, family dining lounges with kitchenettes, business centers and the chapel. Baylor Plano president Jerri Garison reports, "I have heard from many patients that they feel like they are in a hotel, not a hospital. The clinical staff would tell you that the design is very functional for them. They love this hospital."

Clockwise from below: Patient room, medical office building with overhead pedestrian walkway, dining facility, healing garden

Opposite top, left to right: Operating room, reception/concierge desk, corridor

Photography: Craig Blackman

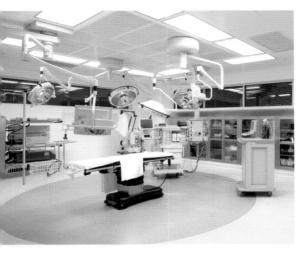

Left: Entrance at front of exterior at twilight

Above: Back of exterior

Right: Back of exterior

Opposite top, left to right: Entry lobby, lobby, patient room

Photography: Art Gray

With the July 2010 opening of the 370,000-square-foot Chickasaw Nation Medical Center, on a 230-acre wooded site in Ada, Oklahoma, Chickasaws and other Native Americans in eastern Oklahoma gained access to a unique facility that celebrates Chickasaw heritage while supporting state-of-the-art healthcare. The new Center, designed by PageSoutherlandPage, is three times larger than the Carl Albert Indian Health Facility it replaces, and features a 72-bed, three-floor, 218,000-square-foot hospital, two-story, 141,100-square-foot outpatient clinic, and 11,500-square-foot central utility plant. Its design sensitively blends Native American culture with modern healthcare. For example, since Native Americans profoundly respect nature, the building highlights views of the creek, specimen trees and other pristine elements on the former agricultural site. Similarly, the floor plan connects to the site as much as possible by relegating service functions to the sides rather than the back, and the Chickasaw emphasis on giving, sharing and connecting to the extended family is embodied in the "Town Center" atrium at the heart of the facility. Noting the priority Chickasaws assign to health care, Bill Anoatubby, governor of the Chickasaw Nation, declared, "This medical center is designed and equipped to empower our staff to offer the highest level of health care."

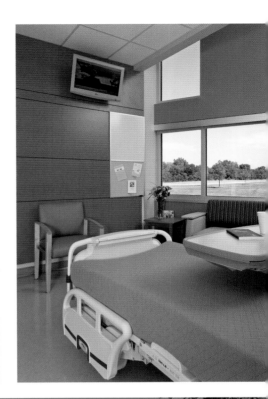

PageSoutherlandPage

Norman Regional Health System
The HealthPlex
Norman, Oklahoma

People in Norman, Oklahoma recognize the 152-bed HealthPlex, featuring cardiovascular services, spine and orthopedic surgery, and women's and children's services, by its bold, contemporary elevator tower and high perch on Interstate 35. Norman Regional Health System's newest facility serving south central Oklahoma, the eight-story, 398,598-square-foot structure was designed by PageSoutherlandPage as a state-of-the-art showcase for three centers of excellence, the Heart and Vascular Institute, Women's and Children's Pavilion, and Orthopedic Center, which connect to a curving spine on a 95-acre site that includes two medical office buildings and parking garage. The HealthPlex offers an exceptional, patient-centered healing environment. The two-story, glass-enclosed lobby greets patients and visitors, who may take a grand stair to dining on the garden level below. In addition, the interior boulevard provides access to care destinations and amenities; social spaces invite patients, visitors and staff to nurture relationships; family spaces encourage family participation in caregiving; and private patient rooms based on the Planetree model support patient empowerment. Describing his involvement in developing HealthPlex, Norman Regional's vice president Daryle Voss noted, "Being part of a project that will improve the overall quality of life in Norman and the surrounding community for decades to come has been very rewarding."

Top, left to right: Women's and Children's Pavilion reception, patient room, waiting area

Right, far right: Dining, healing garden

Opposite: Exterior at main entrance

Photography: K.O. Rinearson; McNeese, Fitzgerald Associates

PageSoutherlandPage

Scott & White University Medical Center
Round Rock, Texas

Left: Atrium lobby

Above: Exterior

Below: Main concourse

Photography: Peter Hoffmann, AIA/PageSoutherlandPage, Richard L. Muniz

Offering heart and vascular, orthopedic, diagnostic imaging, women's and children's services, Scott & White University Medical Center has opened an impressive, 76-bed, four-story, 193,000-square-foot, technologically-advanced community hospital, three-story, 81,000-square-foot clinic/medical office building and 6,800-square-foot central plant on a 68-acre campus in Round Rock, Texas. The Center introduces Scott & White Health Care, the largest multi-specialty practice in Texas and clinical educational partner for Texas A&M Health Science Center College of Medicine, to Central Texas' fast-growing healthcare market. The spacious, sunny and open facility, designed by PageSoutherlandPage, gives Scott & White an easily navigable, patient-centered environment that meets three strategic goals. Besides incorporating evidence-based design to promote quality patient care and attract superior personnel, the new facility reinforces Scott & White's distinctive architectural brand, established by PageSoutherlandPage at the main campus in Temple, and anticipates future growth to a 300-bed hospital with additional MOBs. The hospital anchors the campus with a main concourse connecting all major destinations, positioning facilities like the cafeteria, gift shop and central elevator for central locations after expansion. Not only are Central Texas' residents receiving state-of-the-art care here now, they can expect uninterrupted service even as a new expansion, designed by PageSoutherlandPage, targets future needs.

Perkins Eastman

115 Fifth Avenue • New York, NY 10003 • 212.353.7200 • 212.353.7676 (Fax)

www.perkinseastman.com

Perkins Eastman

Duke University Hospital Emergency Department
Durham, North Carolina

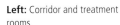

Left: Corridor and treatment rooms

Lower far left, lower left: Triage desk, pediatric ED lobby

Bottom far left, bottom left: Pediatric treatment room, entrance lobby

Below: Covered entryway

Photography: Eduard Hueber/ Arch Photo, Robert Benson

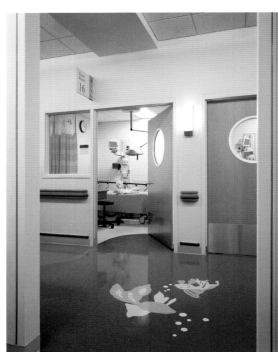

An emergency department that excels at being patient- and family-friendly as well as efficient recently opened at Duke University Hospital, Duke University Health System's flagship teaching hospital, in Durham, North Carolina. Designed by Perkins Eastman, the award-winning one-floor, 41,500-square-foot renovated and expanded ED comprises 85 treatment rooms, four triage rooms and 7,000-square-foot ambulance bay. A Level I trauma center, it is flexible enough to handle worst-case scenarios, maintains separated yet connected adult and pediatric EDs, and offers good wayfinding. Arriving patients are immediately comforted by the 6,000-square-foot, double-height and extensively glazed entrance lobby and waiting area, which can function independently as a treatment area, thanks to hidden headwalls, sinks and 100 percent exhaust air. The adult ED enhances staff efficiency and maximizes patient privacy as a linear model ED, placing public circulation on the periphery to provide quiet, secure patient spaces, and separating the staff core to preserve patient treatment confidentiality. For individualized care of children, the 4,900-square-foot pediatric ED assembles around a central core nursing and support area, allowing a clear view of patient treatment and circulation spaces. Consequently, the hospital is pleased to report the upfront waiting line is dramatically shorter and overall throughput is more efficient.

Perkins Eastman

Memorial Sloan-Kettering Cancer Center Surgical Platform
New York, New York

Technically speaking, Memorial Sloan-Kettering Cancer Center's award-winning new one-floor, 70,000-square-foot surgical pavilion, in New York, comprising 21 state-of-the-art operating rooms, 52-bed PACU, pre-surgical center, conference center and support areas, is not floating on air. However, since MSK's midtown Manhattan campus lacked available space, the design by Perkins Eastman hovers "in the sky" as a massive, table-like steel superstructure, supporting its "super truss" top at the 9th floor level on legs formed by trussed columns piercing through the working hospital. The surgical pavilion is equally innovative. Its OR suite attaches five mini-suites, each typically clustering four smart ORs around a sterile core, to a central spine corridor. The central spine, envisioned as a "Fifth Avenue" entryway at the surgeons' request, extends a warm welcome to staff and patients through generous dimensions, barrel-vaulted ceilings, wall sconces, artwork and high-end finishes. Public spaces, including waiting area, family amenities and consultation rooms, are conveniently located and appointed in warm and soothing colors, attractive furnishings such as beech wood paneling, translucent glass, upholstered lounge seating, and art. Not to be overlooked, staff spaces stand apart from public spaces and surgical suites, giving hospital personnel the respite they need as much as anyone else.

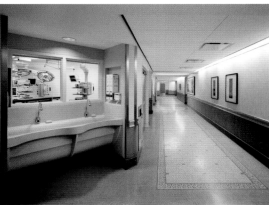

Above right, right: Dining, central spine
Below: PACU
Lower left, bottom left: Waiting area, nurses station
Opposite: Waiting area
Photography: Chuck Choi

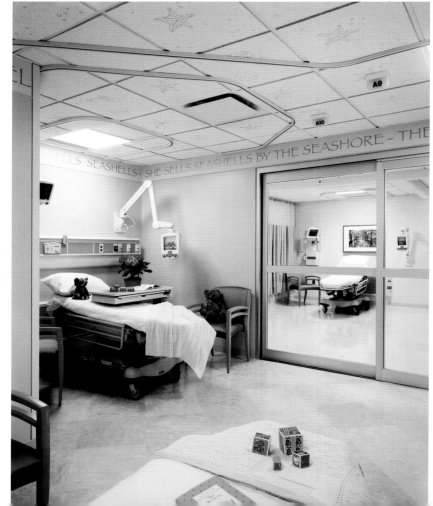

Perkins Eastman

Queens Hospital Center
Ambulatory Care Pavilion
Jamaica, New York

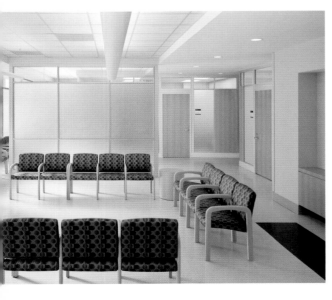

Queens Hospital Center's elegant new six-story, 144,000-square-foot Ambulatory Care Pavilion, in Jamaica, New York, is one of numerous improvements maximizing patient convenience and positive outcomes for residents of southeastern and central Queens. Its completion significantly enhances the adjacent 279-bed municipal hospital. The facility centralizes outpatient facilities for primary care, pediatrics, behavioral health, dialysis, dental and eye care and houses administrative, educational and training facilities for the entire Center. The pre-cast concrete structure designed by Perkins Eastman places patients, visitors and staff in a life-affirming environment that reduces stress, supports efficiency and accommodates change. A key to its success is clear organization. A 300-foot-long glazed public concourse on the southern perimeter anchors the interior, linking all clinics to the staff and service elevator core on the west and public elevator core to the east, and providing a light-filled, two-story atrium and public entry plaza at the eastern side. With strongly delineated public and private zones guiding them, patients and families find wayfinding excellent. The Center's executive director Antonio Martin praised Perkins Eastman for designing "a sophisticated, aesthetically enhanced and inviting structure that will vastly improve both access and quality of care for the more than 135,000 New Yorkers we serve each year."

Left, top to bottom: Pediatric waiting, examination room, primary care waiting

Below: Public concourse

Opposite: Exterior at public entry plaza

Photography: Paúl Rivera/ ArchPhoto

Perkins Eastman

Al Maktoum Accident and Emergency Hospital
Dubai, United Arab Emirates

Can a facility provide state-of-the-art treatment and technology for minor- to high-level trauma accidents and emergencies while taking a compassionate, non-institutional approach to healthcare design? That has been the goal of the Dubai Health Authority in commissioning Perkins Eastman to design the new, 300-bed, four-story, 95,000-square-meter Al Maktoum Accident and Emergency Hospital, in Dubai, United Arab Emirates, which comprises an inpatient unit, clinical space, emergency department and dedicated support area. Ground-level and rooftop helipads and an ambulance receiving area are directly linked to the trauma resuscitation suite, operating area and diagnostic imaging unit with X-ray, CT and MRI capabilities, as befits a trauma center. However, most spaces are arrayed around the central atrium that constitutes the "spine" of the building and provides direct access to all medical departments. To ensure patients a natural and soothing experience, the design also incorporates interior and exterior landscaped courtyards with water features, quality building materials such as wood, stone, resilient sheet flooring, solid counters and sink surfaces,

and fritted glass, and fine furnishings combining comfort, durability and hygiene. With thoughtful planning like this, Al Maktoum Accident and Emergency Hospital can readily embrace both cutting-edge medicine and patients' and families' needs.

Above: Exterior
Right: Atrium
Below: Site plan
Illustrations: Courtesy of Perkins Eastman

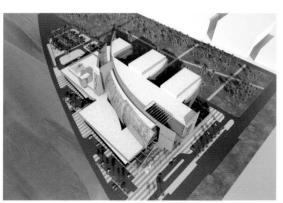

Perkins+Will

Atlanta • Boston • Charlotte • Chicago • Dallas • Dubai • Hartford • Houston • London
Los Angeles • Miami • Minneapolis • New York • Orlando • Philadelphia • Research Triangle Park
San Diego • San Francisco • Seattle • Shanghai • Toronto • Vancouver • Washington, DC

Perkins+Will

Mayo Clinic Replacement Hospital
Jacksonville, Florida

The Mayo Replacement Hospital is located on the same site as Mayo's outpatient, research and educational facilities. The new hospital has 214 beds in a 670,000 square foot, 6-floor tower connected to the existing Mayo building. A sweeping canopy marks the main entry to the hospital and provides clear wayfinding. The main lobby provides a timeless and gracious setting for admissions, benefactor recognition and heritage artifacts displays. The large, light-filled private patient rooms are designed to make a hospital stay more pleasant for patients and their families including large windows, seating areas and sofa beds. Beyond its pleasant, sunny waiting area, the emergency department has a centralized team work area and private treatment rooms that feature rich colors, patterns and soft lighting. The new surgical suite contains 16 oversized inpatient operating rooms built around a sterile core. Mayo's long history and experience in healthcare buildings informed a design philosophy that maximizes flexibility. Future expansion of the facility could reach 550 beds and 16 stories. A master plan for the location and size of public corridors maintains clear wayfinding and connection between buildings. Separation of public and staff/support circulation provides a framework for future expansion without disrupting existing efficiencies.

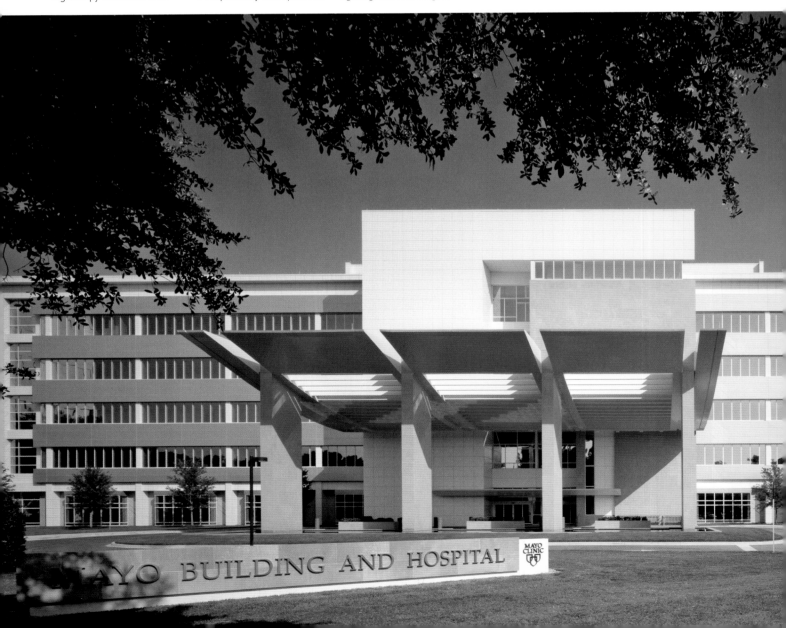

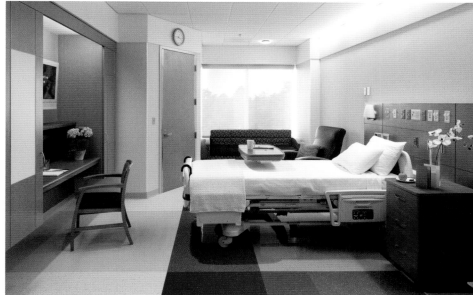

Top left: Lobby

Left: Exterior with entrance canopy

Top: Patient floor lounge

Above: Patient room

Photography: Nick Merrick/ Hedrich Blessing; Anton Grassl/ Esto Photographics

Perkins+Will

Saint Joseph's Healthcare
Diagnostic Imaging Department
Hamilton, Ontario, Canada

A visit to a hospital's imaging department is frequently disorienting, stressful and uncomfortable for patients and their families. At St. Joseph's Healthcare, a 650-bed hospital, in Hamilton, Ontario, Canada, patients will be pleasantly surprised by the new Diagnostic Imaging Department, designed by Perkins+Will. The one-story, 27,000-square-foot facility consolidates six previously independent modalities into a single new imaging center.

Located primarily below grade, the department has minimal access to natural light and views. The design blurs the line between nature and nurture, giving everyone who experiences the space a sense that nature surrounds them at all times. The "spa-like" environment uses materials such as topiary trees set into a bed of river rock, wood, stone, glass etched with tree imagery, landscaped murals and back-lit ceiling images. A straight-forward floor plan promotes

intuitive way finding and a clear division between public and private functions. Despite budgetary constraints, the new facility improves efficiency and amenities for staff and accommodates the latest state-of-the-art imaging technologies. The new department enables St. Joseph's to continue providing superior care and making a difference in healthcare delivery in Ontario for generations to come.

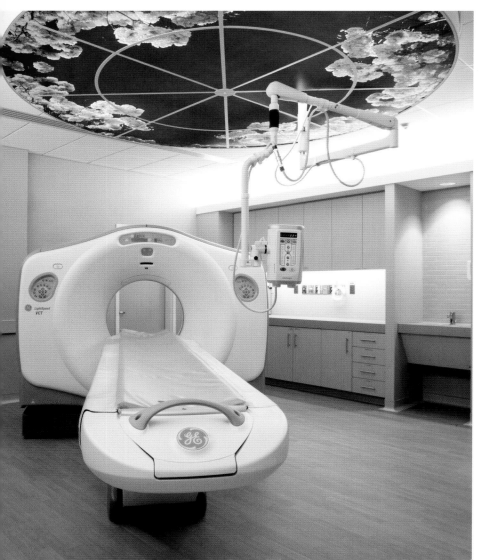

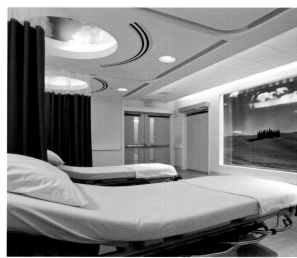

Above: Subwaiting area

Right: Registration

Opposite bottom left: CT procedure room

Opposite bottom right: Holding area

Photography: Peter A. Sellar Photography, Inc.

Perkins+Will

Mattel Children's Hospital UCLA
Los Angeles, California

Ranked among the world's elite institutions for pediatric research, teaching and care, Mattel Children's Hospital UCLA serves over 6,000 inpatients and 100,000 outpatients annually as "a hospital within a hospital" at Ronald Reagan UCLA Medical Center, in the Westwood district of Los Angeles. Recently, it moved to a new, 520-bed replacement hospital along with Ronald Reagan UCLA Medical Center and the Stewart and Lynda Resnick Neuropsychiatric Hospital at UCLA. The 90-bed (including 24-bed PICU and 22-bed Level III NICU), 122,041 square foot Mattel Children's Hospital UCLA has been designed to treat children ranging in age from newborn to 17 years old in an exceptional, family-focused environment where families are welcomed as care givers. Inspired by "Children Around the World," the design fills diagnostic and treatment facilities as well as patient rooms and family areas with a child-friendly décor that balances natural light and space with privacy. The new facility offers patient rooms that accommodate families and include day beds for overnight stays, Child Life activity rooms for specific age groups and a large fifth-floor terrace bordering the activity rooms that gives children direct access to the outdoors.

Top: Activity room
Left: Nurse station
Below: Labor and delivery room
Opposite: Child Life entry
Photography: Benny Chan/fotoworks

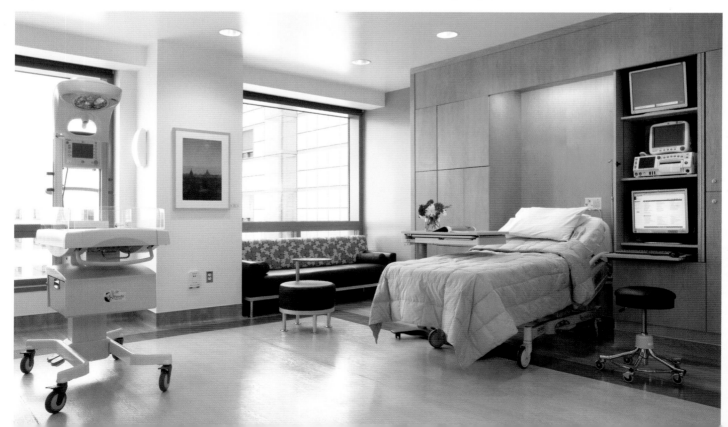

Perkins+Will

Mount Sinai Medical Center
Jaffe Food Allergy Institute
New York, New York

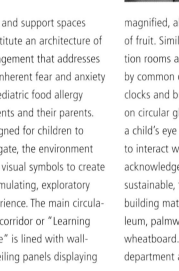

The Jaffe Food Allergy Institute at New York's Mount Sinai Medical Center was established in 1997 to combine world-class clinical and laboratory research programs. A recent, one-floor, 3,500 square foot renovation of the clinical areas greatly enhances patient care. New examination and consultation rooms, food challenge/treatment rooms, offices, conference rooms, reception area and support spaces constitute an architecture of engagement that addresses the inherent fear and anxiety of pediatric food allergy patients and their parents. Designed for children to navigate, the environment uses visual symbols to create a stimulating, exploratory experience. The main circulation corridor or "Learning Spine" is lined with wall-to-ceiling panels displaying magnified, abstracted images of fruit. Similarly, examination rooms are identified by common objects such as clocks and buttons etched on circular glass panels at a child's eye level. The need to interact with food is even acknowledged through such sustainable, food-based building materials as linoleum, palmwood and wheatboard. Mount Sinai department administrator Megan Morgan observes, "Patients come in and are pleased with the aesthetic, so it has been a great morale booster and workspace improvement."

Above: Learning Spine

Far left and left: Examination room, corridor window

Photography: Dub Rogers/Dub Rogers Photography

200

RTKL Associates Inc.

1717 Pacific Avenue • Dallas, TX 75201 • 214.468.7600 • 214.468.7601 (Fax)

www.rtkl.com

RTKL Associates Inc.

West Chester Medical Center
West Chester, Ohio

West Chester Medical Center in West Chester, Ohio, is a new-market hospital planned and designed by RTKL to provide state-of-the-art facilities now and allow seamless expansion later. The 160-bed, five-floor, 389,000 square foot facility is the most technologically advanced hospital in greater Cincinnati.

It is master planned for a future parking garage, a second MOB, and another bed tower, which will bring the hospital to a total of 300 private patient rooms. Centralized and decentralized nurse work areas provide the advantages of both care models, and a first-of-its-kind patient-nurse communication

system integrates the staff's wireless VoIP phones into the nurse call system for instant connectivity. The nurse call system also utilizes touch screens in each patient room. Retail design principles were used to enhance wayfinding and customer service. Every area of the hospital is easily accessible from

the rotunda at the main entrance, and the physical environment is soothing and relaxing. Amenities include a walking path, workout areas for staff and visitors, and large patient rooms that can accommodate family members. "Starting with the architectural layout," notes Carol A. King, senior

vice president of the Center, "every aspect of the hospital maximizes patient and family comfort and convenience."

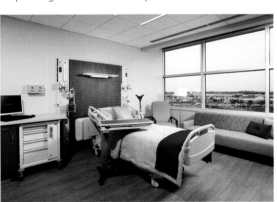

Above left: Atrium gallery
Above: Exterior at main entrance
Far left: Patient room
Left: Patient floor lobby
Opposite: Rotunda atrium
Photography: Jeffrey Totaro

RTKL Associates Inc.

Catholic University of Korea
Seoul St. Mary's Hospital
Seoul, South Korea

To create a state-of-the-art academic medical center with an exceptional healing environment, Seoul St.Mary's Hospital, an affiliate of Catholic University of Korea's prestigious medical school, asked RTKL to make improvements to a design already under construction. The resulting 1,200-bed, 28-level, 1.9-million square-foot facility, designed by SAMOO, architect of record, and RTKL, design advisor, now incorporates features that dramatically increase its effectiveness. RTKL recognized the necessity of multi-bed wards in Korea, but redesigned the wards for flexibility so that every room module can accommodate a five-bed, two-bed, or one-bed ward. Because multi-bed wards cannot comfortably accommodate visitors, RTKL added day rooms where patients and families can visit. Operating theaters arranged in rosettes, Korea's traditional OR layout, were modified to support a more flexible process and to better separate clean and soiled items. And in the Emergency Department, the patient experience and caregiver efficiency were improved by creating distinct paths for differing patient populations. Pediatric patients are separated from trauma patients, for example. Even the hospital's exterior was redesigned to project a more upscale, contemporary appearance with metal panel and glass curtain walling accentuating the hospital's high-tech nature while terracotta and granite convey a sense of warmth and strength.

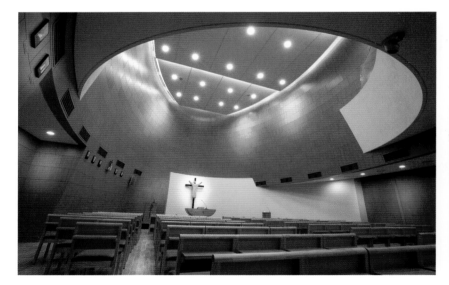

Top left: Nurse station, VIP ward
Top right: Exterior
Above: Chapel
Left: Pediatric waiting
Opposite: Atrium
Photography: © Jae Moon Lim

204

RTKL Associates Inc.

Banner Del E. Webb Medical Center
Patient Care Tower
Sun City West, Arizona

Additions can update hospitals as well as increase their capacities and capabilities, and the new Patient Care Tower at Banner Del E. Webb Medical Center, in Sun City West, Arizona, does so in award-winning style. Designed by RTKL Associates, the 72-bed, six-story, 180,000-square-foot addition introduces a new main entrance and lobby along with the patient wing and 43-station emergency department. The design incorporates various innovative concepts that enhance public perception of the 404-bed institution. In public areas and private patient rooms, hospitality-style ambiance is sustained with appropriate furnishings, desert-inspired colors and local materials to calm and comfort patients and visitors. Public and private circulation are separated to improve operational flows without cross traffic. Landscaping, highlighted by a Reflection Garden featuring native plants, combines with artwork, all-private patient rooms and family amenities to advance the healing environment. To project a modern look that complements existing structures, the architecture articulates its contemporary forms in the colors and materials of older construction—while capturing sunlight and minimizing heat gain. Voicing her appreciation, Becky Kuhn, Banner Del Web's CEO, observes, "This new wing introduces our community to a variety of evidence-based design features that promise better patient outcomes, patient safety and patient experiences."

Below: Lobby

Right: Healing garden

Far right: ED examination room

Below right: Exterior at main entrance

Photography: © dimitre.com

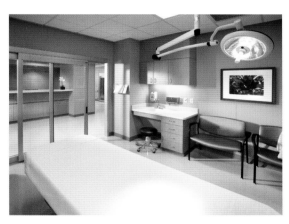

RTKL Associates Inc.

Children's Medical Center Dallas
Tower 3B Interiors
Dallas, Texas

The new 11-story, 389,463-square foot Tower 3B at Children's Medical Center Dallas is a recent addition to the hospital. RTKL was the interior designer for the new tower with FKP as architect of record. The tower's two-story atrium lobby has a fiber-optic star ceiling with large sculptural pendant lights that resemble moons floating in space.

Nebula Chroma, a custom-designed mosaic mural, creates an intriguing focal point in the atrium. Below the mural, an elliptically-shaped grand staircase suggests the curves of the hospital's logo, a balloon on a string. In fact, stylized versions of the logo can be seen throughout the hospital in a looping ribbon motif like the one on the glass of

the staircase railing. Also in the lobby, an interactive art wall provides an entertaining and safe play area for children. Family lounges on each patient floor include glass mosaic fireplaces, and a curving soffit with twinkling lights stretches into the corridor beyond. On the NICU floor, wood and frosted glass sliding panels separate patient bays and provide

privacy, infection control, and give staff easy access to the adjacent bay. Indirect lighting protects babies' sensitive eyes, while natural light and cycled lighting helps develop their circadian rhythms.

Below left: Atrium lobby
Below right: NICU bay
Bottom left: Interactive art wall
Bottom right: Family lounge
Photography: © Charles Davis Smith, © RTKL/Michael Cagle

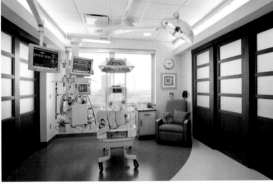

Sparling

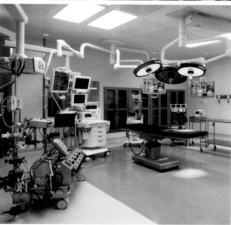

Seattle, WA • Portland, OR • San Diego, CA • Houston, TX

800.667.0610 • 206.667.0554 (Fax)

www.sparling.com

Sparling

Sacred Heart Medical Center at RiverBend
Springfield, Oregon

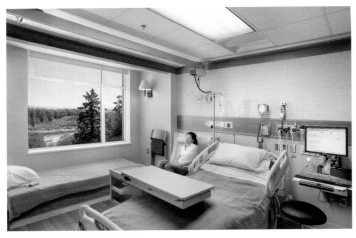

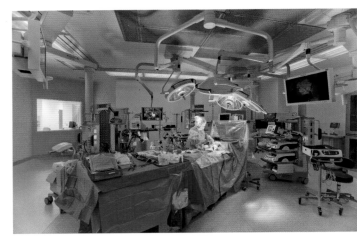

From refrigerating medications to powering lasers for heart surgery, keeping the electricity flowing is essential to the new Sacred Heart Medical Center at River Bend, in Springfield, Oregon, designed by Anshen + Allen Architects with Sparling as electrical engineer and technology infrastructure designer.

A comprehensive, advanced yet patient-friendly, 386-bed, eight-story, 1.2 million-square-foot replacement hospital occupying a 181-acre site near the banks of the McKenzie River, Sacred Heart at RiverBend is designed with power systems that can remain intact and operational in a flood. To meet this

challenge, Sparling analyzed the McKenzie River floodplain as well as the histories of flood-prone hospitals before persuading the hospital that the electrical equipment should be located on the fourth floor. The unconventional, award-winning design sets the standard for health-care facilities in flood-prone

areas by ensuring that the operations of institutions like Sacred Heart at RiverBend, whose appealing, national park lodge-style healing environment incorporates the findings of evidence-based design, are not jeopardized by floodwaters. "Sparling's insight into the future of technology and flexible,

adaptable design concepts have helped us design a state-of-the-art facility that is poised to serve the region for the next 100 years," concludes Jim Weston, director of facilities management, PeaceHealth Oregon region.

Top left, right: Patient room, operating room

Left, above: Exterior, corridor with screens

Opposite: Fireplace lobby

Photography: Denny Sternstein

Sparling

Swedish Medical Center
Swedish Orthopedic Institute
Seattle, Washington

The first dedicated facility of its kind in the Pacific Northwest and one of the largest in America, Swedish Medical Center's new Swedish Orthopedic Institute, on the Center's downtown Seattle campus, offers comprehensive orthopedic services in an efficient, patient-

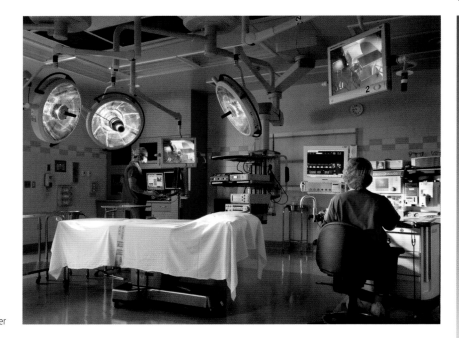

Right: Operating room

Far right: Exterior

Below: Pre-operative/recovery area

Photography: Ben Benschneider

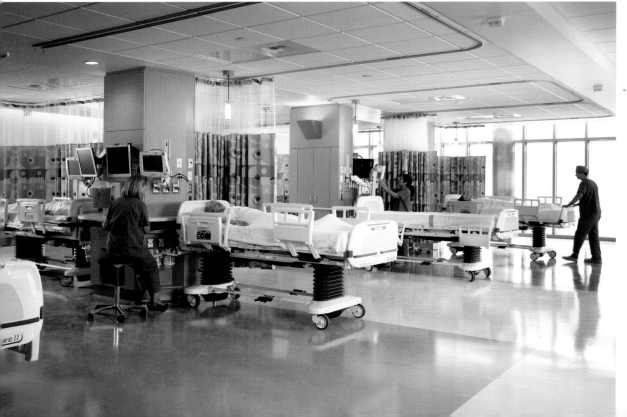

centered environment. The 84-inpatient-bed, nine-story, 372,000-square-foot building, designed by NBBJ with electrical, technology and acoustics design by Sparling, comprises a surgical pavilion, medical office/inpatient tower and various transparent public spaces and connectors. In designing the emergency power distribution system, Sparling discovered the available and owner-preferred equipment would not let the system comply with the newly adopted National Electric Code 2005. Sparling subsequently adapted the "line reactor" technology typically used to slow electrical current in variable speed drives and motors to serve the building's electrical fault current issues. By conscientiously addressing the complexities of the new technology application, modeling to prove the innovative concept would work, and negotiating the fast-track construction, shipment and inspection of the huge custom reactor, Sparling successfully managed the award-winning project, satisfying the Center and the NEC. Darren Redick, the Center's former vice president, facilities, praised Sparling, saying, "Your team collaborated with the entire design team to bring state-of-the-art systems and efficient, cost-effective design solutions to our project."

Sparling

Sutter Medical Center Castro Valley
Castro Valley, California

Discussions about a replacement hospital for Eden Medical Center, in the San Francisco Bay Area's Eden Township, first surfaced in the late 1990s, precipitated by legislation enacted after the Northridge earthquake damaged several hospitals so severely that their operations were curtailed—and by concern over Eden's aging facility. Today, a new, 130-bed, nine-story, 224,500-square-foot regional hospital, Sutter Medical Center Castro Valley, is rising on the Eden campus in Castro Valley, designed by Devenney Group with comprehensive technology planning, design and coordination by Sparling. To meet a project goal to reduce current hospital operational costs by at least 30 percent, Sparling has developed a solution to streamline the design and building systems. Key aspects include: eliminating three initially desired systems while keeping their features by leveraging other key systems, promoting system integration, and leveraging systems with each other; providing cost efficiencies using procurement strategies focused on qualified vendors who can provide multiple systems; establishing integrated infrastructures to allow multiple systems to utilize a single common infrastructure rather than propriety infrastructure; and introducing an integration strategy of systems with EPIC, an electronic medical records system, as a platform to automate workflow and use systems as automation tools. The facility opens in 2013.

Above left, right: Patient room
Left: Exterior
Below: Waiting room
Opposite: Nurses station
Illustration: Courtesy of Devenney Group

Sparling

Methodist Willowbrook Hospital Expansion
Houston, Texas

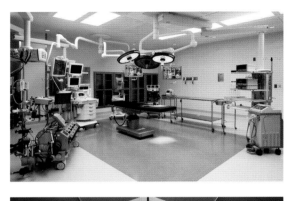

In May 2010, a major expansion on the 52-acre Houston campus of Methodist Willowbrook Hospital doubled the size of the nonprofit, tertiary care hospital. The new, seven-story, 496,000-square-foot North Pavilion and 67,000-square-foot renovation were designed by Parsons with technology programming and design services by Sparling. Besides housing the new Heart and Vascular Center, Stroke Center, imaging services, operating rooms, cardiac catheterization labs, pharmacy, laboratory, chapel and full-service cafeteria, the North Pavilion enabled the emergency department to expand to 28 beds and offer dedicated pediatric rooms and fast-track rooms for minor emergencies. Sparling collaborated with the Methodist Hospital System to provide technology visioning to drive the strategic analysis of systems and process selection. Working with the design team, it created designs that were cost effective, flexible and expandable to meet current and long-term needs, providing consulting/design services for data center layout, wireless LAN, distributed antenna systems, personal communications systems and patient entertainment/education systems. Appropriately, Sparling found that close integration with the IT department, researching legacy systems' capabilities and potential upgrades to ensure seamless information transfer between old and new systems, was key to integrating technology systems in new and existing facilities, preparing Methodist Willowbrook for its centennial in 2019.

Top: Operating room

Above: Atrium lobby, North Pavilion

Left: North Pavilion exterior

Photography: Richard J. Carson Photography, AZ Photography

TAYLOR

2220 University Drive • Newport Beach, CA 92660 • 949.574.1325 • 949.574.1338

www.TAA1.com

TAYLOR

Miller Children's Hospital
Pediatric Inpatient Addition
Long Beach, California

Rising like a castle from a rocky shoreline in Long Beach, California, the new four-level, 120,000-square-foot Pediatric Inpatient Addition at Miller Children's Hospital glows like a beacon, fulfilling goals set for its design by TAYLOR with expertise and imagination. The Addition provides state-of-the-art diagnostic and treatment spaces, including pediatric surgery with 18-bed PACU, pediatric imaging, 48-bassinet (24 built, 24 shelled) Level III NICU, and 24-bed pediatric nursing unit, that are part of a joyful healing environment sustained by such patient- and family-focused spaces as the entrance lobby, reception, sibling playroom, family resource center, conference/education center,

retail shop, sanctuary, staff support space, family support space and garden waiting area. The thematic vision of the "Hero's Journey" and "Castle Refuge" that helps the facility engage and comfort stems from a remarkable community visioning process to describe children's triumph over illness and injury. Youngsters immediately relate to the facility when they see such imagery as the first floor lobby's "shore" of beach umbrellas, arcades and boardwalk shops. "TAYLOR sought to know what people were passionate about," observes Richard DeCarlo, COO, Miller Children's Hospital. "Then, they embraced that and were able to achieve a design that really brought us beyond architecture."

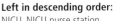

Left in descending order: NICU, NICU nurse station, surgery stairs and family waiting, main lobby

Below: Exterior at dusk

Opposite top, left to right: Sanctuary, pre-surgery waiting, lobby play area

Photography: Assassi Productions

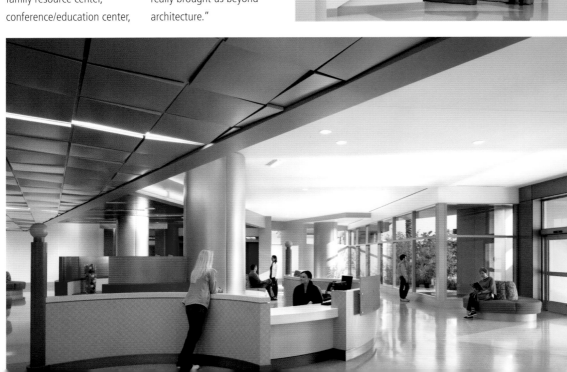

TAYLOR

Kaiser Permanente Los Angeles Medical Center
Rejuve(n)ate Café
Los Angeles, California

A hospital's plan for a prominent street presence along fabled Sunset Boulevard in the Hollywood district of Los Angeles sounds like wishful thinking—until visitors and staff at Kaiser Permanente Los Angeles Medical Center discover the new Rejuve(n)ate Café. This one-level, 16,062-square-foot cafeteria with outdoor terrace, exhibition cooking, servery and kitchen, designed by TAYLOR, has transformed an existing medical record storage facility into a staff and visitor amenity whose sloping and undulating 30- to 35-foot-high storefront inserts an eye-catching break within a five-block-long medical campus boundary. Set between a new replacement hospital to the west and an existing medical office building to the east, the Café pairs its sleek curtainwall exterior with a high-end retail interior. Modern furnishings in clean and informal lines, playful colors, and sophisticated lighting, combining daylight with LEDs and a programmable lighting system, complement an interior where transparent, resin-formed "clouds" and other organic forms contrast with stainless steel food service equipment to create a fresh, airy and sophisticated neighborhood coffee shop. Less conspicuous but equally functional is the Café's role as an extension of the existing pedestrian concourse between campus buildings, which the structure accommodates with 22-foot-high open ceilings. The coffee's hot—and the café too.

Upper left: Main servery area

Far left, left: Perimeter seating, curtainwall detail

Above: Sunset Boulevard perspective

Opposite bottom, left to right: Exhibition cooking, coffee bar, lounge seating

Photography: Jonnu Singelton Photography

220

TAYLOR

Kaiser Permanente
Palm Court II Call Center
Fontana, California

Kaiser Permanente recognized its new Palm Court II Call Center, in Fontana, California, would be large. However, the national healthcare provider approached the fast-track development of its new medical business and call center, transforming an abandoned concrete tilt-up retail "big box," determined to create a work environment where the staff could find a sense of place, identity and belonging instead of the all-too-common stress. The one-story, 150,000-square-foot warehouse has become a two-story, 197,000-square-foot service center for 17 different service departments, providing three call centers, training center, employee lounges, coffee bar, conference center, patient support services, patient business services, pharmacy administration, education and training, recruitment services, and medical administrative service areas. Yet the facility resembles a metaphorical "village," complete with its own internal "streets" connecting department "neighborhoods," "parks" and "community centers," thanks to a multi-layered design based on thoughtful planning, clear circulation, and a lively visual vocabulary of street light fixtures, street signs, street furniture, vibrant artwork, natural lighting and uniquely fashioned and richly colored architectural facades. In fact, the Center's young workers genuinely like the edgy contemporary design.

With staff retention up and stress levels down, they report that their "village" is thriving.

Above right, right: Mezzanine lobby, conference center
Below left, below: Coffee bar, call center
Opposite: Main lobby
Photography: Mike Torey Photography

Conference Room
Extended Care &
Geriatric Services
Home Care Services
Outside Utilization
Restrooms

TAYLOR

St. Jude Medical Center
Northwest Tower
Fullerton, California

Timeless modern design and timely economic feasibility have powerfully shaped the new 120-bed, four-level, 200,000-square-foot Northwest Tower at St. Jude Medical Center, in Fullerton, California, a design-build replacement hospital designed by TAYLOR as part of the master plan for St. Jude's 14.7 acre campus. Guided by a Project Design Charter to provide a functional facility that placed priority on the future needs and technology for staff and patient care, TAYLOR designed a structure both straightforward and economic to build yet befitting a major urban medical center. Efficient and functional, the Northwest Tower also incorporates evidence-based design to improve patient services. For example, nursing floors embrace the "racetrack" configuration with private patient rooms on the perimeter. Patient rooms designed with in-board bathrooms in order to maximize patient exposure to daylight and nature with views to a healing garden courtyard.

Decentralized nursing work areas are accompanied with centralized patient care nursing areas—centralized provides peer interaction and collaboration between physicians, nurses, dietary, social workers and case managers, while decentralized work alcoves allow the caregivers more personal and casual time with the patient. The concept provides a comprehensive level of patient care. The community will find a warm welcome here.

Top left: Staff courtyard entry
Top right: Birdseye view
Above: Northwest campus view
Illustrations: Courtesy of TAYLOR

WHR Architects

WHR Architects   Jersey Shore University Medical Center
Northwest Pavilion
Neptune, New Jersey

For over a century, Jersey Shore University Medical Center, in Neptune, New Jersey, has been serving central and southern New Jersey, evolving from a community hospital into a regional teaching hospital. Now, through a comprehensive, long-term expansion, it calls Transforming Care: The New Jersey Shore, the Center is combining advanced medicine with evidence-based design to create an exceptional patient experience. The completion of the six-floor, 433,400-square-foot Northwest Pavilion, designed by WHR Architects, is described by Steven Littleson, president of the Center, as "a key step in the evolution of our vision to become best teaching hospital in New Jersey." Besides providing a 144-bed patient care pavilion featuring all-private rooms grouped into innovative 12-bed nursing care "neighborhoods," the project includes a state-of-the-art diagnostic and treatment building, surgical suites, 12-bed ICU, and emergency department and Level I trauma center for treating 100,000 patients annually. Sophisticated technology is integrated into a sustainable facility (the East Coast's largest LEED Gold certified hospital and New Jersey's First LEED Gold Certified health care facility) that welcomes and supports patients and visitors alike. Its healing environment—featuring good wayfinding, attractive settings, home-like furnishings, high quality lighting, and art—extends from radiant public spaces such as the entrance, four-story atrium and healing gardens to all clinical areas.

Above left: Corridor
Above: Nurses station
Below: Lounge
Below left: Exterior with new entrance
Bottom: Surgical suite
Opposite: Atrium
Photography: John Woodruff, Peter Brown/Woodruff & Brown Photography

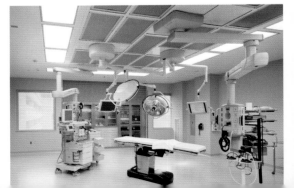

WHR Architects   Oklahoma Heart Institute
Tulsa, Oklahoma

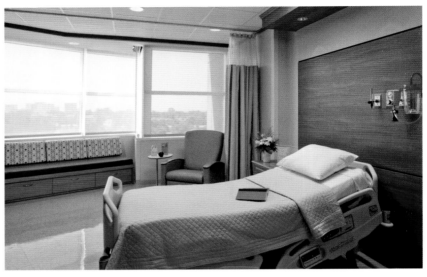

You cannot miss the Oklahoma Heart Institute when you enter the Hillcrest Medical Center campus, in Tulsa, Oklahoma. The largest, most comprehensive hospital of its kind in the state, combining the expertise of eminent cardiologists, endocrinologists and cardiovascular surgeons with the latest in cardiovascular technology to provide superior care, the Oklahoma Heart Institute resides in a newly expanded and renovated structure that stands as a monumental glass beacon of hope and assurance. The 203,000-square-foot project, designed by WHR Architects, represents Phase I of an extensive, ongoing project, and includes such new or remodeled facilities as the entry atrium, 104 all-private beds, six catheterization laboratories, cardiovascular diagnostic center, cardiovascular interventional unit, education center, café and other amenities. Besides establishing its striking new image, the design addresses such broad objectives as upgrading the patient experience through a warm, patient-focused healing environment, providing an efficient, flexible and state-of-the-art workplace for physicians, nurses and support staff, and incorporating sustainable design features wherever feasible, including minimal footprint, maximum daylight in patient rooms and work areas, and materials chosen for long life. Of course, transforming the building into an iconic entry portal to the campus also reflects a deliberate choice—as well as a highly successful one.

Upper left: Tower promenade
Above: Patient room
Left: Exterior
Below: Cardiac CT
Photography: Joe Aker/ Aker/Zvonkovic Photography

WHR Architects   Platte Valley Medical Center
Brighton, Colorado

Platte Valley Medical Center is a community hospital in Brighton, Colorado with far-reaching capabilities—and the desire to grow in a competitive market. On its new 50-acre campus, visible from I-76, the Center has opened a 98-bed, 217,000-square-foot replacement hospital, featuring 28 medical/surgical/pediatric beds, 20 post-partum, six LDR, eight CCU and eight telemetry rooms, 55,000-square-foot medical office building and central plant, designed by WHR Architects as architect of record with Fentress Architects as associate architect. Though the campus will ultimately accommodate a 300-bed hospital and three medical office buildings, the Center already boasts one of Colorado's most comprehensive, fully-integrated wireless hospital systems. In addition, it expands patient care options with a Level IV trauma center, cardiac catheterization laboratory, expanded heart program and Colorado's only Level II special care nursery with eight private rooms for at-risk infants, through a special arrangement with The Children's Hospital. But the Center represents more than advanced technology. Reinforcing its commitment to patient- and family-centered care, it provides a comprehensive healing environment featuring single patient rooms spacious enough for families and friends, waiting rooms with fireplaces where families can relax, and public spaces with materials, furnishings and colors that extend a warm welcome.

Below left: Entry lobby
Below: Patient room
Below middle: Dining room
Bottom: Nurse station
Photography: Joe Aker Aker/Zvonkovic Photography

WHR Architects

Memorial Hermann Healthcare System Community Replacement Hospitals
Katy, Texas and Sugar Land, Texas

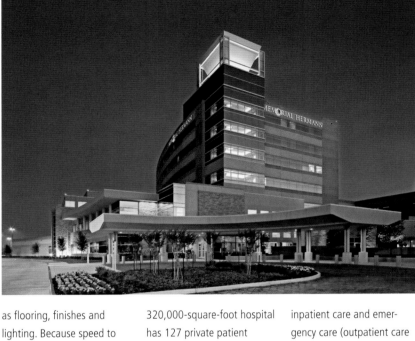

As two of the fastest-growing communities in suburban Houston with substantial demand for healthcare services, Katy, Texas and Sugar Land, Texas have been excellent locations for Memorial Hermann Healthcare System to build new replacement hospitals. The development of the two facilities, designed by WHR Architects, has been particularly noteworthy because both began in the same time frame with a prototype that was adapted to meet the specific demands of their communities. Although the use of a prototype is unusual for a not-for-profit healthcare system, the design similarities of Memorial Hermann Katy Hospital and Memorial Hermann Sugar Land Hospital provided numerous benefits. Memorial Hermann Healthcare System exploited the prototype to capture cost savings in design and construction and to establish "best practices" for such building materials as flooring, finishes and lighting. Because speed to market was a factor—design and construction took 30 months—the prototype facilitated decision-making through the use of common elements, including basic layout, functional relationships, architectural features and mechanical systems. Program differences were driven primarily by each community's needs and site adaptation. For example, Katy's seven-story, 320,000-square-foot hospital has 127 private patient rooms, while Sugar Land's five-story, 223,000-square-foot hospital has 77 private patient rooms. More significant are the shared values. The two hospitals embrace a core philosophy developed by Memorial Hermann Healthcare System and WHR Architects that promotes a patient-centric, latest-in-technology and healing environment. While each provides state-of-the-art inpatient care and emergency care (outpatient care is offered at the freestanding medical office buildings on hospital grounds), what patients probably notice first are interiors designed to make the hospital experience quiet, relaxing and enjoyable, in direct contrast to the busy hustle outside. Both hospitals feature two-story, hotel-like atriums, high ceilings in the public concourse and lobbies, dining areas overlooking outdoor terraces and healing

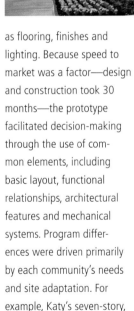

Above: Main entrance and illuminated sky top (at Katy, like other views on this and facing pages)

Above left: E-bar

Left: Care team station

Far left: LDRP room

Opposite: Public concourse

Photography: Joe Aker/Aker/Zvonkovic Photography

WHR Architects

gardens, private patient rooms with guest sleeping accommodations, family activity areas, educational libraries, meditation rooms, warm colors and lighting, rich wood, stone and tile finishes, and wayfinding graphics. Similarly, WHR Architects has employed architecture to define a memorable, signature identity for each hospital's exterior, shaped by such elements as the curved bed tower, entrance canopy and tall, lantern-like tower, which acts as a landmark and source of inspiration day and night. Public response to the new facilities has been dramatic. To quote Marilyn Paine, chief nursing officer of MH Katy Hospital, "We have seen a huge improvement in our patient satisfaction scores."

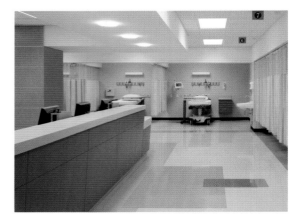

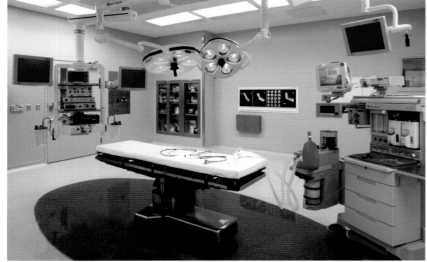

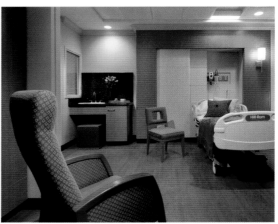

Clockwise, from left: Lobby with fountain, OR, PACU, VIP patient room (all at Sugar Land)

Wilmot Sanz, Inc.

18310 Montgomery Village Avenue, Suite 300 • Gaithersburg, MD 20879 • 301.590.2900 • 301.590.8150 (Fax)

www.wilmot.com

Wilmot Sanz, Inc.

Howard County General Hospital:
A Member of Johns Hopkins Medicine
Columbia, Maryland

The opening of the New Patient Pavilion at Howard County General Hospital: A Member of Johns Hopkins Medicine, in Columbia, Maryland, marks another distinguished milestone in Wilmot Sanz's ongoing service to the Hospital since 1995 as architect, master planner, programmer and interior designer. Opened in 1973 as a 59-bed, short-stay hospital, the 227-bed comprehensive, acute-care medical center is working with Wilmot Sanz to implement a Campus Development Plan that accommodates an expanding and aging population and increasing admissions and

emergency department visits. The 90-bed, five-story, 104,000-square-foot addition and 123,000-square-foot renovation establishes a modern image for the hospital and creates a healing environment based on transitional interiors and abundant natural lighting. Among the key features are three floors of new, all-private patient rooms with distinct zones for patients, family members and staff (ongoing renovations will refit the older patient tower to create 62 private beds from existing semi-private rooms), new critical care floor, new main lobby with convenient access

to outpatient services, including new gymnasiums for cardiopulmonary and newly centralized adult and pediatric rehabilitation, and

redesigned surgical services, laboratory and pharmacy. Its sophisticated, hospitality-inspired setting has been a welcome sight to residents

of this rapidly growing community in suburban Maryland.

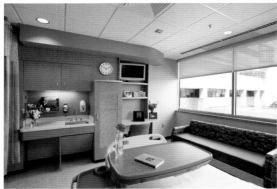

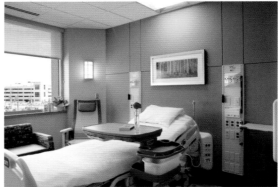

Above: Main lobby

Far left: Patient room

Left: Patient room

Lower far left: Nurses station

Lower left: Lounge/family waiting

Opposite: Exterior

Photography: Paul Burk Photography

234

Wilmot Sanz, Inc.

Shady Grove Adventist Hospital
Rockville, Maryland

When Shady Grove Adventist Hospital, part of the Adventist HealthCare system, began serving the residents of Montgomery County, Maryland and surrounding areas in 1979, it was surrounded by fields. Thirty years later, the 320-licensed bed hospital is encircled by buildings in the Washington suburb of Rockville, and has celebrated its third decade by completing a new patient tower, combining a five-story, 222,000-square-foot expansion and 58,000-square-foot renovation, designed by Wilmot Sanz. In implementing the first phase of a long-range master plan, the facility brings a new approach to patient care—the Planetree model—along with 90 medical/surgical beds, 48 post-partum beds and 32-bassinet NICU stations, a 20-operating room surgical suite, an emergency department addition, and a new, two-story main entrance atrium. Configured for private patient rooms, a staff/patient care core absent the traditional nurse station, and residentially appointed family spaces with kitchenettes and computer touchdown work areas, the patient floors follow the Planetree model in giving patients choices in nurturing care, active involvement, family support and privacy. Interiors enhance this decentralized, informal and home-like atmosphere with such details as comfortable transitional furnishings, wood grain and other nature-inspired finishes, daylight and lower lighting levels, a healing environment worthy of the hospital's 30th anniversary.

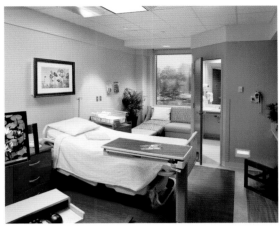

Far left, left: Patient room, family lounge and nurse team station

Below: Building exterior and front healing garden

Opposite top: Porte cochere

Opposite bottom: Patient unit reception

Photography: Michael Dersin Photography, Wilmot Sanz (exterior)

Wilmot Sanz, Inc.

Provena Saint Joseph Hospital
Elgin, Illinois

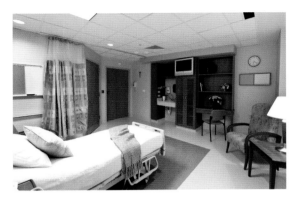

For over 100 years, Provena Saint Joseph Hospital, in Elgin, Illinois, has been a major care provider in the Fox River Valley, absorbing advanced treatments and technologies to provide leading-edge care, and expanding and renovating facilities to serve a dynamic population. A recent development involving a four-story, 164,000-square-foot addition and 96,000-square-foot renovation, designed by Wilmot Sanz, has produced a new, all-private, 99-bed patient tower, main lobby, dining room, café and gift shop, along with major facelifts for the critical care unit, imaging department, surgery department—which added five surgical rooms and three catheterization laboratories, including one hybrid OR/cath lab—and doctors' lounge. The project enhances hospital capabilities in diverse ways. Each patient room, for example, offers space for visitors, hotel-like décor and a flat screen television. The innovative hybrid OR/ catheterization laboratory delivers "all-in-one-room care," having all the needed technology on hand and interventional cardiologists, vascular interventionalists and surgeons readily available for a quick transition between catheterization and surgical procedures. Total joint replacement and arthoscopic procedures can now be performed in the new state-of-the-art surgical suites, in addition to open heart procedures in the updated cardiovascular surgical suite. The hospital's dedication to patients is flourishing in its second century.

Wilmot Sanz, Inc.

Inova Health System
Dewberry Life with Cancer® Family Center
Fairfax, Virginia

What could easily be mistaken for a grand country residence in a transitional architectural style is actually Inova Health System's new Dewberry Life with Cancer® Family Center, in Fairfax, Virginia, a beacon of enlightenment and assurance to cancer patients and their families in northern Virginia. The resemblance is deliberate, of course. A freestanding resource center combining the comforts of home with a place for cancer education and support of cancer patients and survivors, the two-story (plus basement), 16,900-square-foot structure was designed by Wilmot Sanz to consolidate the functions of Inova's Life with Cancer® program, which has been helping people for over 20 years to face the challenges of this complex disease. Within a rustic exterior of stone, brick and glass, the interior combines wood panels, trim and flooring, porcelain tile, warm, earth tones, and residential-style furnishings and lighting fixtures to create stylish and inviting rooms for art therapy, meditation, counseling, reading, exercise, diet education, digital information resources, community meetings and the popular Complimentary Therapy programs. The new Family Center allows the Life with Cancer staff to continue their important work in a comforting, soothing environment that promotes healing outside the confines of a hospital.

Above: Reception lounge with community great room beyond

Left: Entrance to children's wing

Far left: Resource library

Below: Exterior

Photography: Paul Burk Photography

Landscape Architects

*E*vidence-based design tells us that patients enjoying a connection to nature experience faster and more effective healing. Fortunately, nature can be incorporated in the healthcare facility in many ways. How effective the nature connection can be is highlighted by the healing garden, designed for therapeutic purposes. Open lawns, for example, can readily host social gatherings and large group activities, while smaller, enclosed garden "rooms" serve individuals and small groups. Plantings, building materials and water features can stimulate the senses by encouraging touching, smelling and hearing. Walks, ramps, stairs and lawns can place patients in real-life mobility conditions. The landscape architecture firms featured in the following pages showcase some of the varied roles nature is playing in today's healthcare environment.

Healthcare Spaces No.5

Dirtworks Landscape Architecture, PC

200 Park Avenue South • New York, NY 10003 • 212.529.2263 • 212.505.0904 (Fax)

www.dirtworks.us

Dirtworks Landscape Architecture, PC

Elizabeth & Nona Evans Restorative Garden
Cleveland Botanical Garden
Cleveland, Ohio

An integral component of Cleveland Botanical Garden's mission is to help "people of all ages, backgrounds and abilities appreciate and benefit from the positive role that plants play in their lives." The new, award-winning, 12,000-square-foot Elizabeth & Nona Evans Restorative Garden, designed

Clockwise from upper left:
Stone walk with pool, welcome area, Contemplative Garden's overlook, garden path and water feature, secluded seating area

Opposite upper right: Water feature in Demonstration/ Exploration Garden

Photography: © Dirtworks, PC

244

by Dirtworks Landscape Architecture, creates a private environment within a public garden setting for visitors with special physical and psychological needs. Dirtworks' scheme skillfully exploits the small, sloped and circumscribed space. Adjoining a busy dining terrace as the primary view from the Botanical Garden's gracious library, it unfolds as three unique settings. The Contemplative Garden, contained by a stone walk leading to a lawn panel, seating areas, water features and overlook, provides a quiet entry point to all three gardens. By contrast, a high stone wall defines the Demonstration/Exploration Garden, offering patients opportunities for touching, smelling and hearing through cascades and niches of plants and water features that include a waterfall, pool and water trickling over moss-covered stones. Patients with severe disabilities likewise appreciate the Horticultural Therapy Garden's generous choice of planter widths, heights and special displays for crafts and other activities. Brian Holley, the Garden's Executive Director, praises the "highly functional yet extremely personal and deeply emotive" design.

Dirtworks Landscape Architecture, PC

Natural Science Courtyard at the Science Center
Keene State College
Keene, New Hampshire

To develop a "learning courtyard" for Keene State College's newly expanded and renovated Science Center in Keene, New Hampshire, Dirtworks Landscape Architecture worked closely with Mitchell/ Giurgola Architects and Banwell Architects, the building's architects, Keene State's Dean of Sciences and faculty members from the geology, astronomy and botany departments. The resulting 7,850-square-foot Natural

Science Courtyard not only connects the 93,640-square-foot Science Center to the school's arboretum and gardens, but it also acts as a model outdoor field laboratory, incorporating elements of the natural landscape without replicating it. Geology is the unifying element, expressed through a cross-courtyard paving pattern and boulders from the surrounding region, with stone chosen for

its aesthetics, geological significance, and durability as paving. Plants are also essential to the design. Because the building's north-south orientation provides distinct microclimates for plant displays, a large spectrum of plants has been selected to illustrate the evolution of New Hampshire flora, providing an important demonstration of seasonal change, plant growth and maturity. For Gordon

Leversee, Dean of the School of Sciences and Social Sciences, the courtyard creates a space that invites students, staff and visitors to "come informally to reflect on beautiful surroundings that resonate with the rich landscape of New Hampshire."

Right, far right: Diagonal main path representing geologic strata, aerial view of courtyard showing three ecosystems: mature woodland, woodland edge and hedgerow/meadow

Top of pages, left to right: View of courtyard through grove, intersecting paths displaying geologic strata and volcanic activity, woodland edge, meadow and hedgerow

Photography: © Andrew Bordwin

Dirtworks Landscape Architecture, PC

Monter Cancer Care Center
North Shore – Long Island Jewish Health System
Lake Success, New York

Patients are delighted to encounter flourishing groves of bamboo inside the new Monter Cancer Care Center, in Lake Success, New York. The 37,000-square-foot cancer outpatient facility, part of North Shore-Long Island Jewish Health System's Center for Advanced Medicine, occupies a converted historic warehouse that uses three original, 120-foot-long skylights to add the restorative qualities of nature as a complementary healing force to clinical treatment. As the first phase of a new comprehensive care center, designed by EwingCole with Dirtworks Landscape Architecture as landscape architect, the space features a series of atria, reception and waiting areas along a spacious corridor called "Main Street." The indoor planting of bamboo along the 1/8th-mile-long corridor parallels the outdoor planting of birch trees. While the birch trees define entry points, screen out traffic and frame views of the surrounding landscape, staggered bands of bamboo create lush, serene settings for relaxing and quiet conversation. Equally important, the award-winning landscape installation addresses the concern that overexposure to bacteria carried in plants and soil could harm some patients undergoing treatment. Submerging the plants beneath a protective strata of black river pebbles and landscape fabric, flush with the adjacent pavement, effectively shields patients from possible soil contaminants.

Above: Staggered bands of bamboo create settings for relaxing and quiet conversation

Photography: © Barry Halkin

Dirtworks Landscape Architecure, PC

Joel Schnaper Memorial Garden
ArchCare/Terence Cardinal Cooke Healthcare Center
New York, New York

Since 1995, the Joel Schapner Memorial Garden has assumed a unique role at ArchCare/Terence Cardinal Cooke Healthcare Center, a continuing care facility in New York for 700 residents comprising the elderly and people with developmental disabilities and chronic illnesses, including HIV. The restorative garden's 3,000-square-foot rooftop space represents an oasis of peace and tranquility for residents and visitors alike as well as a venue for social and therapeutic activities ranging from plant cultivation to parties and exercise classes. So when the roof's waterproofing membrane needed replacement in 2005, the

Center asked Dirtworks Landscape Architecture to design a replacement garden retaining its basic design using more durable materials. The design provides spaces of varying degrees of enclosure and privacy that are flexible in size and arrangement. Highlights include protective settings ranging from tents and tree canopies to fully open areas, vine-covered lattice panels that screen mechanical equipment, create privacy between activities, and display art and craft exhibits, and practical, sturdy and low-maintenance accessories and materials, such as fiberglass circular planters supporting mini-gardens. At the reopening,

Mimi Fierle, Director of the Center's therapeutic recreation department, described the garden as "a source of joy, delight and inspiration for our residents and their families."

Above left, right: Patient and caregiver enjoying the garden together, one of many clear views that let staff relax while monitoring groups and activities

Left: Lattice columns and vine-covered trellises frame views and spaces

Photography: © Bruce Buck

Dirtworks Landscape Architecture, PC

Health Center
The Center for Discovery
Harris, New York

Located on 350 acres in Harris, New York, the Center for Discovery offers individuals with multiple disabilities and medical frailties and their families innovative education, clinical and social experiences that enrich their lives through personal accomplishment. Its belief that environmental health influences community health is reflected in its two-story, 28,000-square-foot Patrick H. Dollard Health Center, a diagnostic and treatment facility designed by Guenther 5 Architects (now Perkins+Will), and the ongoing remediation and transformation of its former industrial agricultural site, which Dirtworks Landscape Architecture serves as landscape architect. To expand on the sustainable building practices embodied by the award-winning steel-and-wood building, Dirtworks worked with clinicians, nurses, teachers and residential staff to develop opportunities for individuals with medical frailties to enjoy nature through outdoor activity and education areas, walking trails, wildlife and native plant enhancement programs. In such projects as master planning for a new campus for children with autism, Family Resource Center, Dance Barn and new adult housing, the vernacular landscape is used to define entries and circulation and to frame and screen views. Besides linking the Center's buildings to the overall campus, the evolving landscape is encouraging individuals to engage with nature, to learn and to explore.

Below: The sweeping, open meadow before the Patrick H. Dollard Health Center

Photography: © David Allee

Mahan Rykiel Associates, Inc.
Landscape Architecture, Urban Design and Planning

800 Wyman Park Drive, Ste. 100 • Baltimore, MD 21211 • 410.235.6001 • 410.235.6002 (Fax)

www.mahanrykiel.com

Mahan Rykiel Associates, Inc.

University of Maryland Medical Center Weinberg Addition, Interior Healing Garden, Surgical Waiting Area and Atrium
Baltimore, Maryland

An impressive new addition to the University of Maryland Medical Center downtown Baltimore campus is the 375,000-square-foot Harry and Jeanette Weinberg Building. Designed by Kohn Pedersen Fox as design architect, Perkins+Will as medical planner, DCI as architect of record, and Mahan Rykiel Associates as landscape architect, the striking, modern structure houses new and expanded facilities for cancer patients, adult and pediatric emergency departments, diagnostic imaging, food court, chapel, patient resource center and employee learning center. Its innovative architecture is matched by outstanding landscape architecture in its interior healing garden, surgical waiting areas and seven-story atrium spanning the space between the new building and an adjacent older one. The interior landscaping features seating clusters divided by trees and low plantings. Raised planting areas create the soil depth necessary for tree plantings, define seating clusters, and suggest privacy for visitors. Tree species were selected for their ability to form spaces or create screening from above. Located near surgical suites, these planted waiting areas offer a gentle respite from the stressful hospital environment. In evaluating the landscape design, Jeni Wright, the Center's project manager, remarked, "Its success can be measured by the use it receives from staff, patients and visitors."

Below left: Atrium
Below: Sitting area in atrium
Bottom: Healing garden
Photography: Patrick Ross

Mahan Rykiel Associates, Inc.

Kennedy Krieger Institute
Outpatient Center, Therapeutic Garden
Baltimore, Maryland

Improving the lives of children and adolescents with brain and spinal cord disorders and injuries since 1937, Baltimore's Kennedy Krieger Institute serves over 13,000 individuals annually through inpatient and outpatient clinics, home and community services and school-based programs. Its new Harry and Jeanette Weinberg Outpatient Center is a six-story, 15,000-square-foot facility, designed by Stanley Beaman Sears with Mahan Rykiel Associates as landscape architect, which consolidates all outpatient services. The sleek and largely transparent structure and graceful, oasis-like therapeutic garden simultaneously supports the programs of the clinical staff and showcases the facility's mission to the community. A gracefully curving fountain wall defines the 20,000 square foot garden which is comprised of smaller walled 'rooms' designed for individuals and small groups. Among the many features of the garden are multi-seasonal plantings, grading challenges such as steps and ramps, and varied paving materials designed to stimulate the senses and provide opportunities for real-life mobility conditions. Water features which encourage playful interaction are accessible to children and to individuals in wheelchairs. Karen Good, Kennedy Krieger's manager of training and clinical education, applauds the garden's scheme, saying, "Therapists are natural explorers; they are accustomed to using their environment. I think a therapist will look at this and know exactly what to do with it."

Clockwise from right: Aerial view, active play area, evening view of building and garden, child and parent at fountain

Photography: Kennedy Krieger Institute, Jim Roof/Stanley Beaman Sears

Mahan Rykiel Associates, Inc.

Mercy Medical Center
Mary Catherine Bunting Center at Mercy
Baltimore, Maryland

Among the amenities awaiting patients, families and staff at Mercy Medical Center's new 18-story, 686,000-square-foot Mary Catherine Bunting Center, on Mercy's downtown Baltimore campus, are three rooftop gardens. Program elements included providing outdoor places of respite for hospital staff, visitors and patients, and coordinating these spaces with appropriate clinical units in the facility. Designed by Ellerbe Becket with Mahan Rykiel Associates as landscape architects, the roof gardens beautifully satisfy this program element, but the team faced a number of challenges in doing so. Located on the 8th (maternity) and 9th (ICU) floors, the gardens provide generous usable space but also required careful planting and berming to shield adjacent patient rooms from visitors to the garden. Other considerations included creating areas with sufficient soil depth for tree plantings and on-going coordination with structural engineers. As it implements a long-range strategic plan for campus modernization, Mercy Medical Center, a Catholic healthcare facility and teaching hospital for the University of Maryland School of Medicine founded in 1874, has generously planted gardens where a parking garage once stood.

Clockwise from top right:
8th-floor gazebo, aerial view of 8th and 9th floors, street perspective of building and gardens, 8th floor garden in evening view

Photography: Patrick Ross

Illustration: Courtesy of Ellerbe Becket

Mahan Rykiel Associates, Inc.

Anne Arundel Medical Center
Healing Garden and Koi Pond
Annapolis, Maryland

Many regional medical centers started life at or near their communities' centers, including Anne Arundel Medical Center, founded in downtown Annapolis, Maryland in 1902. However, when the hospital consolidated acute care services in 2001, it relocated to an all-new facility at its suburban Medical Park campus. Among the amenities at the new 316-bed, six-story, 330,000-square-foot Acute Care Pavilion, designed by Wheeler Goodman Masek with Mahan Rykiel Associates as landscape architect, are a healing garden, near the main and ER entrances, and a koi pond, the focal point of the cafeteria garden. The award-winning landscape blends form and function seamlessly. For example, the walkway in the healing garden's narrow, linear space—too tight for a full loop path—diverges in places so visitors need not pass each other, preserving their privacy. Similarly, a rocky stream winds through natural-looking plantings to provide a visible symbol of healing that generates the calming sound of water and thrives as a wildlife habitat. With an entrance only from the building, security cameras disguised as birdhouses and a strategically placed brick wall, the healing garden enjoys visibility with security.

At the Koi Pond, an etched glass railing gives the names of donors subtle prominence. Happily, the hospital's beloved fish are flourishing in their new pond in Medical Park.

Clockwise from below center: Koi Pond planting edge, birds, koi, rocky stream, seating area, view from the cafeteria

Photography: Patrick Mullaly, Joseph Augstein

Mahan Rykiel Associates, Inc.

Providence Hospital
Healing Garden
Washington, D.C.

Chartered by Abraham Lincoln in 1861, 480-bed Providence Hospital is the longest continuously operating hospital in Washington, D.C. and a vital component of Ascension Health, the nation's largest Catholic health system. The venerable institution willingly courts fresh ideas, nonetheless. Its new healing garden, designed by Mahan Rykiel Associates, addresses the needs of the community teaching hospital by providing a meditative outdoor space that simultaneously offers respite from stress and space for outdoor activities such as music concerts and yoga and tai chi classes. A decorative iron picket fence encloses the mostly linear space, and separates the garden from the everyday activity at the hospital's main entrance. The garden is configured as a series of pathways and places with fountains as focal points, seating along the way, a central area with an open lawn, and smaller, contemplative areas that are encircled and protected by lush planting. The garden is presented as a welcoming environment that cleanses, protects and nurtures its occupants. "The garden has been a great success and has been well used by staff, patients and visitors," reports Providence's Thomas Anderson, vice president for facilities management. "We receive many compliments on the garden."

Right: Planting bed and pathway

Below: Fountain and exercise class

Below right: Detail of fountain

Photography: Patrick Ross, Joseph Augstein, G.W. Meredith

Mahan Rykiel Associates, Inc.

Essex County Hospital Center
Cedar Grove, New Jersey

Advances in the medical treatment of mental illness beginning in the 1960s are dramatically portrayed in the newest home of Essex County Hospital Center, in Cedar Grove, New Jersey. A 180-bed, 154,000-square-foot county hospital that houses mentally ill patients, was designed by Cannon Design with Mahan Rykiel Associates as landscape architect. The new construction replaces a much smaller predecessor from 1897. The landscape development of the hospital and its 11-acre campus represented a considerable challenge despite its modern, safe and serene image, due to steep grades across the site, specific outdoor activities that required flat grades, and the need for accessibility. The Hospital Center comprises five interconnected buildings that allow staff and patients to walk throughout the facility without going outside. Indoor spaces include an all-purpose room, residential units, treatment mall and education facilities. Outdoor facilities, include a half-acre courtyard, a greenhouse for therapy, a basketball court, active recreation areas and passive meditative spaces. Careful contouring of the grounds thoughtfully integrates the architectural geometry into the site and creates a series of spaces that enhance the ability of the hospital to serve another century of patients.

Above: Ramp and stairs in courtyard

Above right: Courtyard

Right: Entry plaza

Photography: Courtesy of Cannon Design

257

Mahan Rykiel Associates, Inc.

Master Planning
Fort Benning Replacement Hospital,
Fort Benning, Georgia
Tawam Hospital Master Plan,
Al Aain, Abu Dhabi
St. Luke's Healthcare Village Master Plan
Bethlehem, Pennsylvania

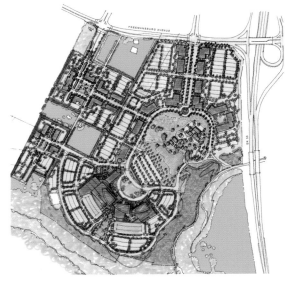

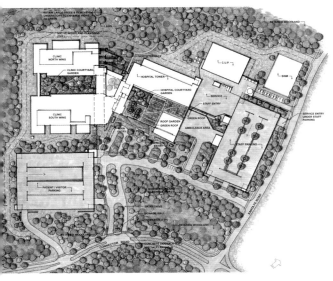

Crafting a workable vision for long-term development forms the core of Mahan Rykiel Associates' master planning for medical campuses. A successful master plan, as created by Mahan Rykiel Associates, is a flexible framework for development that will be implemented over time. Their master plans are based on a thorough understanding of clients' goals tempered by an evaluation of the opportunities and challenges of specific sites. Thus, the master plan for Fort Benning's replacement hospital, designed by Ellerbe Becket (AECOM) with Mahan Rykiel Associates, places a high priority on the beautifully wooded site overlooking the Marne River, in Fort Benning, Georgia, and focuses the entry, patient tower, lobby and dining on views of nature. Likewise, the master plan for the expansion of Tawam Hospital, in Al Aain, Abu Dhabi, developed by RTKL with Mahan Rykiel Associates, arrays the hospital, hotel/conference center, medical school and other components on either side of a huge, river-like water feature. By contrast, landscape amenities introduce village-like characteristics in the master plan for St. Luke's Hospital's Healthcare Village, in Bethlehem, Pennsylvania, a community of wellness where a 600-bed hospital will be accompanied by medical office buildings and support services such as offices, retailing, housing and a hotel/conference center.

Above: St. Luke's Healthcare Village Master Plan

Upper left: Fort Benning Master Plan

Left: Tawam Hospital Master Plan

Illustration: Courtesy of Mahan Rykiel Associates

Wayfinding

ospitals and other healthcare facilities are never truly completed because their technologies, treatments and patient populations are changing constantly. Robotic surgery equipment, for example, is reshaping the operating room. Families, increasingly welcomed as partners in care giving, need overnight accommodations. Aging populations heighten the demand for heart and cancer care. For these and many other reasons, healthcare facilities are forever remodeling and expanding. While these changes do not necessarily compromise the original spatial organization, they make wayfinding programs a necessity. The environmental graphic design firms featured in the following pages employ signage, color coding and other forms of placemaking, wayfinding and environmental graphics to tell patients, families and staff where they're going in the contemporary healthcare facility.

Healthcare Spaces No.5

FMG Design, Inc.

FMG Design, Inc.

Vanderbilt University Medical Center
Monroe Carell Jr. Children's Hospital at Vanderbilt
Nashville, Tennessee

In the six years since the February 2004 opening of Monroe Carell Jr. Children's Hospital at Vanderbilt in Nashville, Tennessee, the 238-bed pediatric care institution has gained recognition as one of America's top 30 children's hospitals in gastroenterology, heart and heart surgery, neonatology, orthopedics and urology by *U.S. News & World Report.* In addition to bringing hope and healing to patients and their families in Nashville and middle Tennessee, the hospital also functions as a teaching and research facility to train future pediatric physicians and improve the nation's medical treatment of children. The hospital's imaginative architecture and interior design, the work of Earl Swensson Associates, support its activities closely, accompanied by a compelling graphics program designed by FMG Design. The graphics meet numerous goals: to stimulate all ages, lower stress levels, promote wayfinding, and connect to the campus of Vanderbilt University Medical Center. Combining vivid imagery, bright and pleasing colors, and attractive, durable forms in acrylic, 3-Form and other materials, the FMG Design program has produced such signature features as "butterfly" and "pencil" donor walls and a playful outdoor illuminated sign bearing the hospital's name at the main entrance, adding award-winning graphics to the hospital's outstanding environment.

Above: Main entrance sign

Far left, left: "Butterfly" donor wall, directional sign

Opposite bottom left, right: "Pencil" donor wall, grand lobby recognition

Photography: Steve Harris

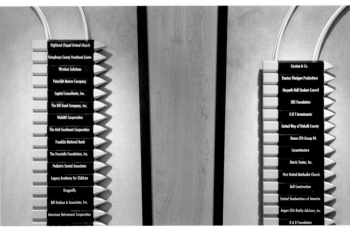

FMG Design, Inc.

Northeast Georgia Medical Center
Gainesville, Georgia

Named one of America's 100 Top Hospitals for 2009 by Thomson Reuters, Northeast Georgia Medical Center, in Gainesville, has delivered expert care since its founding in 1951 that has won acclaim at state and national levels. Citations include a number one ranking in Georgia and top five percent nationwide for cardiac care, a rating in America's top six percent for cancer care, and one of the first in the country to receive stroke specialty care certification for a CARF-accredited inpatient stroke program. As the centerpiece of the Northeast Georgia Health System, a not-for-profit community health system serving nearly 700,000 people in 13 counties in northeast Georgia, the 557-bed Center, designed by HKS, Inc., maintains an extensive campus that draws active support from a program of placemaking, wayfinding and environmental graphics, designed by FMG Design. Asked to develop a clean wayfinding system on difficult terrain for the Center's many connected buildings of varied size, age and design, FMG Design created a comprehensive system employing acrylic, glass, vinyl, wood and stone that has been carefully coordinated with the architecture, interior design, landscaping and lighting. In addition, the program has successfully integrated a major donor recognition program throughout the facilities, including The Medical Center Foundation's prestigious Hall of Honor.

Opposite top: Directional sign

Below clockwise from far left: Hall Of Honor signage system, outdoor directional sign, chapel sign, outdoor sign at night, outdoor sign at main entrance

Photography: Light Sources, Steve Harris

FMG Design, Inc.

Atrium Medical Center
Middletown, Ohio

Clockwise from top right:
Illuminated sign at the main entrance, main lobby sign, time line display, logo on tower, room signs

Opposite top left, right:
Rotunda sign, donor wall signage system

Photography: Steve Harris

When Middletown Regional Hospital recently considered its options for renovation and expansion in Middletown, Ohio, a community it has served since 1917, the highly regarded institution realized that a new building on a new site close to Interstate 75 and Route 122 would be more cost effective, accessible and expandable. The result is the new, 279-bed, five-story, 544,443-square-foot Atrium Medical Center, designed by Earl Swensson Associates, on a 190-acre campus shared with a children's specialty care center, senior residence and YMCA. The replacement hospital represents a major advancement for regional healthcare, expanding the scope and sophistication of medical services and establishing an outstanding family-centered environment. Aiding significantly in the relocation has been the placemaking, wayfinding and environmental graphics program designed for Atrium by FMG Design. Carefully developed to complement the architecture and interior design, the program uses acrylic, glass, vinyl and wood elements to reinforce a sense of place and directional guidance in the facility. Its effectiveness can be witnessed daily, as patients arrive for the family-centered care and advanced technology that Atrium offers, encompassing a full range of services including cardiac care, sports medicine and physical therapy, a multidisciplinary cancer program and a wide array of women's services.

FMG Design, Inc.

University of Texas Health Science Center
Medical Arts and Research Center
San Antonio, Texas

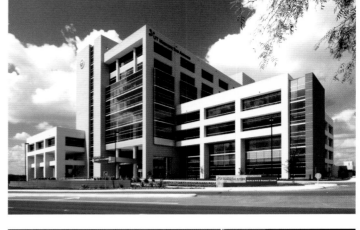

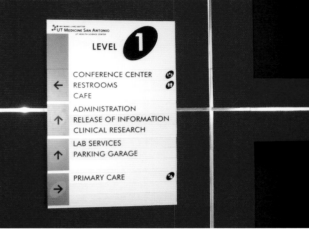

Over 3,000 students annually train with the 600-person faculty of the University of Texas Medical School at the University of Texas Health Science Center at San Antonio, working in a multi-specialty environment that involves more than 100 affiliated hospitals, clinics and health care facilities serving San Antonio and the 50,000-square-mile area of south Texas. For the institution's new, eight-level (plus two-level, 900-car parking garage), 250,000-square-foot Medical Arts and Research Center, designed by FKP Architects, a world-class clinical environment has been designed to house specialty clinics for ambulatory surgery, endoscopy, diagnostic imaging, wellness/rehabilitation, and a women's center, along with other disciplines. The environmental graphics program was meticulously designed by FMG Design to meet the facility's needs. Based on research, analysis, surveying, interviewing and validating, the visual communications system convincingly demonstrates that an effective signing and graphics systems functions not as a separate entity but as an integral part of the built environment. The diligently planned signs and graphics inside and outside of the Medical Arts and Research Center, incorporating a variety of materials such as acrylic and aluminum, not only convey essential information, they also enhance the building's design—saving time and money while enhancing communication and understanding.

Top right: Exterior
Above left, right: Main lobby, directional sign
Below left, right: Outdoor sign, restrooms sign
Photography: Joe Aker

Mitchell Associates

  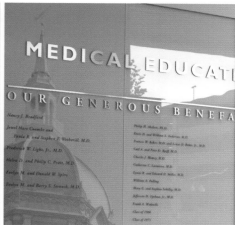

 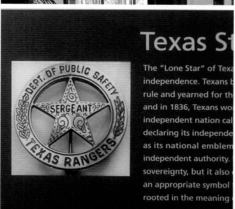 

Mitchell Associates Greenville Hospital System University Medical Center
Greenville, South Carolina

Greenville Hospital System is a not-for-profit academic health organization that operates five campuses providing healthcare across Greenville County, South Carolina and beyond through a tertiary referral and education center, community hospitals, long term acute care hospital, nursing home, outpatient facilities and wellness centers. In coordinating over two million square feet of campus renovation and new construction designed by Design Strategies, Greenville Hospital System retained Mitchell Associates to create a signage color and materials palette to complement its new graphic

and architectural brand standards, and to develop a comprehensive wayfinding and signage standards program for future maintenance and expansion within the Greenville system. Particularly noteworthy are the logistics of the multi-phased (20-plus phases) implementation of interior and exterior signage and specialized graphics across the campuses, and the incorporation of universal healthcare symbols developed by Hablamos Juntos as a system-wide strategy for Limited English Proficient patients and visitors. The success of the program, integrating the grounds and buildings at the Greenville

Memorial Medical Campus, Patewood Medical Campus, Greer Medical Campus, Simpsonville Medical Campus and North Greenville Medical Campus, is evident whenever people consult the distinctive signage and graphics in aluminum, acrylic, vinyl, wood, digital prints, LED lighting and electronic displays.

Clockwise, both pages, from top left: Entrance monument sign, cafeteria entrance sign, stanchion directional sign, directional pylon sign, building identification sign, building identification sign and directional pylon sign, room signage

Photography: Robert Agosta

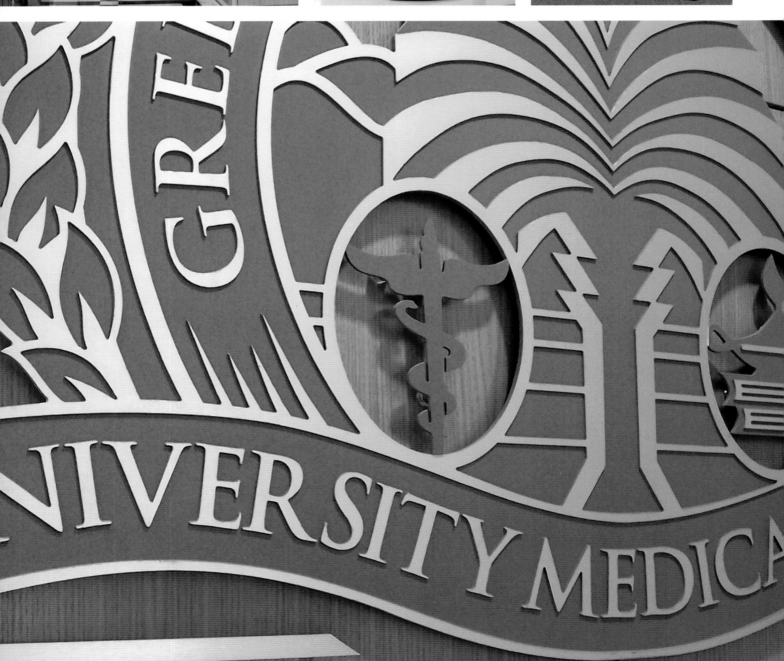

Mitchell Associates

Children's Medical Center Dallas
Dallas, Texas

Clockwise, both pages, from top right: Glass door distraction symbols, elevator lobby interpretive panel detail, donor recognition display, employee recognition display, garage entrance, garage elevator lobby super graphics, exterior directional signage

Photography: Bob Agosta

One of America's largest pediatric healthcare providers, Dallas-based Children's Medical Center is a private, not-for-profit academic healthcare facility dedicated exclusively to the comprehensive care of children from birth to age 18. Children's receives some 360,000 patients annually, providing services ranging from simple eye exams to specialized treatment in areas such as cystic fibrosis. Its main campus, 487-bed, 1.2-million-square-foot Children's Medical Center Dallas, is located in the city's Southwestern Medical District and comprises a hospital, medical office building, surgery center, sky bridges and parking garages. To enhance campus wayfinding, identify buildings and garage levels, and honor donors, Mitchell Associates designed a color coding plan for parking structures, a wayfinding program featuring Texas-themed icons for buildings, connecting bridges, parking decks and floor levels, a Texas-themed donor recognition program, and an elevator identity scheme to link the hospital's existing trainscape entrance brand to wayfinding, working in tandem with the development of a new tower, designed by HKS. The signage, graphics and color coding, taking cues from campus architecture and interior finishes, employ aluminum, acrylic, vinyl, stainless steel, paint, digital printing, glass mosaic tile and LED illumination to alleviate confusion and offer assurance, inspiration and direction to patients, visitors and staff alike.

Mitchell Associates

Johns Hopkins University
Anne and Mike Armstrong Medical Education Building
Baltimore, Maryland

A research university dedicated to advancing the state of human knowledge since its opening in 1876, Johns Hopkins University recently reaffirmed its commitment to teaching and research with the completion of the innovative, four-story, 100,000-square-foot Anne and Mike Armstrong Medical Education Building, designed by Ballinger with wayfinding, signage, graphics, and donor recognition designed by Mitchell Associates, on its East Baltimore campus. The building houses a host of high-tech teaching tools—from plasma screens linked to clinical facilities to virtual-reality surgical simulators—to support a new curriculum called "Genes to Society" that builds on the insights of the Human Genome Project, molecular biology, and genetic biology, using a new method of educating physicians that incorporates medical imaging, virtual-reality simulation, mentoring, small study groups, and collaborative learning. Mitchell Associates' challenge was to create an integrated look with a custom, back-painted glass wall system for a major donor recognition feature, design a custom laminated glass interpretative display panel to architecturally integrate with a custom glass stair rail system, and develop a highly flexible sign system to accommodate changing faculty and class schedules. The design solutions, combining aluminum, acrylic, vinyl, stainless steel, laminated glass and digital printing, perfectly complement the spacious, bold and flexible contemporary architecture.

The School of Medicine extends profound gratitude to those whose contributions are recognized here for advancing the art and science of medical education.

Right, far right: Detail of donor recognition wall

Below: Donor recognition wall

Opposite above: Interpretive display

Opposite below, left and right: Room signage

Photography: Steve Yarnall

Mitchell Associates

Holtz Children's Hospital
Miami, Florida

Located at the University of Miami/Jackson Memorial Medical Center, in Miami, Florida, Holtz Children's Hospital has served the community since 1918 as one of the largest children's hospitals in the southeast United States. The institution is renowned for its pediatric specialists, who work in teams to treat children with needs that can be as uncomplicated as routine care or as demanding as life-saving procedures. Because the entrance to Holtz Children's Hospital is only one of several entrances to Jackson Memorial off 12th Avenue, the neighborhood's main thoroughfare, Mitchell Associates was retained to create a landmark entrance arrival graphic that clearly identified the institution and enlivened the existing adjacent plaza. The design of the signage and super graphics draw inspiration from original art created for the hospital by internationally known local artist and donor Romero Britto, resulting in the vivacious and animated supergraphic illustrations, shapes and colors that are applied to the entrance façade, directional signs and columns throughout the plaza space. Thanks to the graphic program, which utilizes aluminum, acrylic, vinyl, paint and digital printing, children and their families have no trouble finding Holtz Children's Hospital at a time in their lives when it may matter more than anything.

Top left: Entrance plaza graphics
Above left, right: Building identification sign, plaza directional sign
Left: Hospital entrance
Photography: Eric Schmitt

276

Leading the Way to *Measurable Improvement*
Through *Building Design*

BETTER.
FASTER.
TOGETHER.

The Center for Health Design's mission
is to transform healthcare environments
for a healthier, safer world through design
research, education and advocacy. Together,
our world-wide community of healthcare
and design professionals is accelerating the pace
of change and improvement in our industry.

Research
Industry-changing data, acquired through
efforts such as our nationally-acclaimed
Pebble Project®, provides the evidence
to support change.

Education
Programs such as the Evidence-based
Design Accreditation & Certification (EDAC)
and publications keep industry practitioners
afloat on healthcare design best practices.

Advocacy
On behalf of the healthcare design industry,
and in the quest for better buildings, our
volunteer councils drive change in facility
guidelines and standards.

THE CENTER FOR HEALTH DESIGN®

Visit www.healthdesign.org/join

Join Us – Become an affiliate member and benefit from discounts on products and fees,
and access to a wide array of networking opportunities.

Index by Project

- A -

Advocate Condell Medical Center, Emergency Department Expansion and Renovation, Libertyville, Illinois, **20**

Advocate Lutheran General Hospital and Advocate Lutheran General Children's Hospital, Patient Care Tower, Park Ridge, Illinois, **44**

Al Maktoum Accident and Emergency Hospital, Dubai, United Arab Emirates, **192**

Alberta Health Services, Peter Lougheed Centre, Calgary, Alberta, Canada, **144**

Alfred I. duPont Hospital for Children, Family Resource Center and Child Life Facility, Wilmington, Delaware, **166**

Arbuckle Memorial Hospital, Sulphur, Oklahoma, **110**

ArchCare/Terence Cardinal Cooke Healthcare Center, Joel Schnaper Memorial Garden, New York, New York, **249**

AtlantiCare, Oncology Center, Egg Harbor Township, New Jersey, **78**

AtlantiCare Regional Medical Center, New Bed Tower and Renovation Atlantic City, New Jersey, **94**

Atrium Medical Center, Middletown, Ohio, **58**

Atrium Medical Center, Middletown, Ohio, **266**

- B -

Banner Del E. Webb Medical Center, Patient Care Tower, Sun City West, Arizona, **206**

Baylor Orthopedic and Spine Hospital at Arlington, Arlington, Texas, **36**

Baylor Regional Medical Center at Plano, Plano, Texas, **178**

Brigham and Women's Hospital, Shapiro Cardiovascular Center, Boston, Massachusetts, **46**

Brown County Community Treatment Center, Green Bay, Wisconsin, **152**

- C -

Catholic University of Korea, Seoul St. Mary's Hospital, Seoul, South Korea, **204**

Cedars-Sinai Medical Center, Samuel Oschin Cancer Center, Los Angeles, California, **120**

The Center for Discovery, Health Center, Harris, New York, **250**

Chickasaw Nation Medical Center, Ada, Oklahoma, **180**

Children's Medical Center Dallas, Dallas, Texas, **272**

Children's Medical Center Dallas, Tower 3B Interiors, Dallas, Texas, **208**

Christiana Project, Helen F. Graham Cancer Center, Cyberknife Facility, Newark, Delaware, **168**

Cisco LifeConnections Health Center, San Jose, California, **158**

Cleveland Botanical Garden, Elizabeth & Nona Evans Restorative Garden, Cleveland, Ohio, **244**

Cleveland Clinic Abu Dhabi Hospital, Abu Dhabi, United Arab Emirates, **98**

Cleveland Clinic, Arnold & Sydell Miller Family Pavilion and Glickman Tower, Cleveland, Ohio, **174**

Community Hospital of the Monterey Peninsula, The Pavilions Project, Monterey, California, **140**

Cooper University Hospital, Pavilion, Camden, New Jersey, **74**

- D -

Duke University Hospital, Emergency Department, Durham, North Carolina, **186**

- E -

Eisenhower Medical Center, Greg and Stacey Renker Pavilion, Rancho Mirage, California, **154**

Erickson Living at Ann's Choice, Community Building, Warminster, Pennsylvania, **164**

- F -

The First People's Hospital, Shunde District, Guangzhou Province, People's Republic of China, **132**

Forest Park Medical Center, Dallas, Texas, **34**

- G -

Geisinger Wyoming Valley Medical Center, Critical Care Building, Wilkes-Barre, Pennsylvania, **92**

Geisinger Wyoming Valley Medical Center, Henry Cancer Center, Wilkes-Barre, Pennsylvania, **95**

Greenville Hospital System, University Medical Center, Greenville, South Carolina, **270**

Group Health Cooperative Bellevue Medical Center, Bellevue, Washington, **70**

- H -

Harford Memorial Hospital, Havre de Grace, Maryland, **162**

Holtz Children's Hospital, Miami, Florida, **276**

Howard County General Hospital: A Member of Johns Hopkins Medicine, Columbia, Maryland, **234**

- I -

Inova Health System, Dewberry Life with Cancer® Family Center, Fairfax, Virginia, **240**

- J -

Jefferson County Health Center, Fairfield, Iowa, **118**

Jersey Shore University Medical Center, Northwest Pavilion, Neptune, New Jersey, **226**

Jill Bruno Orthodontics, Chevy Chase, Maryland, **82**

Johns Hopkins University, Anne and Mike Armstrong Medical Education Building, Baltimore, Maryland, **274**

- K -

Kaiser Permanente Downey, Medical Center, Downey, California, **130**

Kaiser Permanente Los Angeles Medical Center, Rejuve(n)ate Café, Los Angeles, California, **220**

Kaiser Permanente, Palm Court II Call Center, Fontana, California, **222**

Kaiser Permanente West Los Angeles Medical Center, West Wing Tower Addition, Los Angeles, California, **134**

Keene State College, Natural Science Courtyard at the Science Center, Keene, New Hampshire, **246**

Kiowa County Memorial Hospital, Greensburg, Kansas, **106**

- L -

Labette Health, Parsons, Kansas, **112**

LeConte Medical Center, Sevierville, Tennessee, **60**

The Lindner Center of HOPE, Comprehensive Behavioral Healthcare Center, Mason, Ohio, **48**

- M -

Mattel Children's Hospital UCLA, Los Angeles, California, **198**

Mayo Clinic Replacement Hospital, Jacksonville, Florida, **194**

Memorial Hermann Healthcare System, Community Replacement Hospitals, Katy, Texas and Sugar Land, Texas, **230**

Memorial Sloan-Kettering Cancer Center, Surgical Platform, New York, New York, **188**

Methodist Stone Oak Hospital, San Antonio, Texas, **138**
Methodist Willowbrook Hospital Expansion, Houston, Texas, **216**
Mid-Atlantic Skin Surgery Institute, Waldorf, Maryland, **84**
Midwest Medical Center, Galena, Illinois, **62**
Miller Children's Hospital, Pediatric Inpatient Addition, Long Beach, California, **218**
Morristown Memorial Hospital, Gagnon Cardiovascular Institute, Morristown, New Jersey, **90**
Mount Sinai Medical Center, Jaffe Food Allergy Institute, New York, New York, **200**

- N -

Norman Regional Health System, The HealthPlex, Norman, Oklahoma, **182**
North Shore – Long Island Jewish Health System, Monter Cancer Care Center, Lake Success, New York, **248**
Northeast Georgia Medical Center, Gainesville, Georgia, **264**
Nouveau Medispa, Newark, Delaware, **167**

- O -

Obeid Dental, Chevy Chase, Maryland, **86**
Oklahoma Heart Institute, Tulsa, Oklahoma, **228**

- P -

Park Nicollet Melrose Institute, St. Louis Park, Minnesota, **68**
Penn State Milton S. Hershey Medical Center, Cancer Institute, Hershey, Pennsylvania, **28**
Phoenix Children's Hospital Thomas Campus, Phoenix, Arizona, **128**
Platte Valley Medical Center, Brighton, Colorado, **229**
Price Medical, Washington, D.C., **88**
Provena Saint Joseph Hospital, Elgin, Illinois, **238**
Providence Park Hospital, Novi, Michigan, **172**

- Q -

Queens Hospital Center, Ambulatory Care Pavilion, Jamaica, New York, **190**

- R -

Reid Hospital and Health Care Services, Richmond, Indiana, **102**
Renown Regional Medical Center, Reno, Nevada, **104**
Riverside Regional Medical Center, 5 West Inpatient Oncology Center, Newport News, Virginia, **24**
Royal National Orthopedic Hospital NHS Trust, Central London Outpatient Assessment Centre, London, United Kingdom, **143**
Rush-Copley Healthcare Center, Yorkville, Illinois, **18**
Rush-Copley Medical Center, Connecting Entry Atrium and Lobby, Aurora, Illinois, **22**

- S -

Sacred Heart Medical Center at RiverBend, Springfield, Oregon, **210**
Saint Joseph's Healthcare, Diagnostic Imaging Department, Hamilton, Ontario, Canada, **196**
Salem Hospital, Salem, Oregon, **124**
Samsung Medical Center, Samsung Cancer Center, Seoul, South Korea, **72**
Scott & White University Medical Center, Round Rock, Texas, **184**
Seton Medical Center Williamson, Round Rock, Texas, **126**
Shady Grove Adventist Hospital, Rockville, Maryland, **236**
Southcentral Foundation, Primary Care Clinic III, Anchorage, Alaska, **173**

SSM Cardinal Glennon Children's Medical Center, NICU and Surgery Addition, St. Louis, Missouri, **54**
SSM Cardinal Glennon Children's Medical Center, Warner's Corner, St. Louis, Missouri, **56**
SSM St. Clare Health Center, Fenton, Missouri, **114**
St. Anthony Regional Hospital, Surgery Center, Carroll, Iowa, **146**
St. Elizabeth Healthcare, Ambulatory Care Center and Emergency Department, Covington, Kentucky, **26**
St. John's Mercy Medical Center, Children's Hospital, St. Louis, Missouri, **52**
St. John's Mercy Medical Center, Heart and Vascular Hospital, St. Louis, Missouri, **50**
St. Joseph's Regional Medical Center, New Critical Care Building, Paterson, New Jersey, **96**
St. Jude Medical Center, Northwest Tower, Fullerton, California, **224**
Stafford Hospital Center, Mary Washington Healthcare, Stafford, Virginia, **66**
Stony Brook University Medical Center, Major Expansion Program, Stony Brook, New York, **42**
Sutter Medical Center Castro Valley, Castro Valley, California, **214**
Sutter Regional Medical Foundation, Medical Office Building 2, Fairfield, California, **116**
Swedish Medical Center, Swedish Orthopedic Institute, Seattle, Washington, **212**
Swedish Orthopedic Institute, Seattle, Washington, **170**

- T -

Texas Regional Medical Center at Sunnyvale, Sunnyvale, Texas, **38**

- U -

University Hospitals, Rainbow Babies & Children's Hospital, Neonatal Intensive Care Unit, Cleveland, Ohio, **30**
University of Arkansas for Medical Sciences, Bed Tower and Parking Garage, Little Rock, Arkansas, **122**
University of South Florida Health, Byrd Alzheimer's Institute, Tampa, Florida, **100**
University of Texas Health Science Center, Medical Arts and Research Center, San Antonio, Texas, **268**
USMD Hospital, USMD Cancer Treatment Center, Arlington, Texas, **40**

- V -

Vanderbilt University Medical Center, Critical Care Tower, Nashville, Tennessee, **64**
Vanderbilt University Medical Center, Monroe Carell Jr. Children's Hospital at Vanderbilt, Nashville, Tennessee, **262**

- W -

Warroad Senior Living Center, Warroad, Minnesota, **150**
West Chester Medical Center, West Chester, Ohio, **202**
Wilson Medical Center, Neodesha, Kansas, **108**